This 1991 edition published by Portland House,
distributed by Outlet Book Company, Inc., a Random
House Company, 225 Park Avenue South, New York,
New York 10003.

This book was designed and produced by
Todtri Productions Limited
P.O. Box 20058
New York, NY 10023-1482

Printed and Bound in Singapore

Library of Congress Catalog Card Number 90-63352

ISBN 0-517-05668-2

8 7 6 5 4 3 2 1

Author: Ken Schultz
Producer: Robert M. Tod
Designer and Art Director: Mark Weinberg
Editor: Mary Forsell
Typeset and Page Makeup: Strong Silent Type/NYC

TABLE OF CONTENTS

MAP OF 60 GREATEST FISHING LOCATIONS . . . 4

FOREWORD 5

Alagnak River, Alaska 129

Ashuanipi River, Labrador 116

Atlin, British Columbia 76

Attawapiskat River, Ontario 35

Beaverkill River, New York 21

Bermuda 138

Big Sand Lake, Manitoba 67

Boundary Waters Canoe Area, Minnesota 52

Broadback River, Quebec 34

Cabo San Lucas, Mexico 38

Campbell River, British Columbia 14

Chantrey Inlet, Northwest Territories 81

Columbia River, Oregon/Washington 62

Cozumel, Mexico 108

Delaware River, New York/Pennsylvania 84

English River, Labrador 100

Florida Keys, Florida 82

French River, Ontario 90

Gouin Reservoir, Quebec 94

Great Bear Lake, Northwest Territories 124

Great Slave Lake, Northwest Territories 104

Greer's Ferry Lake, Arkansas 74

Kawartha Lakes, Ontario 56

Kentucky and Barkley Lakes, Ky./Tenn. 114

Kepimits Lake, Labrador 60

Lac Beauchene, Quebec 71

Lake Erie, Ohio/Pennsylvania 8

Lake Eufaula, Alabama/Georgia 96

Lake Guntersville, Alabama 16

Lake Kissimmee, Florida 22

Lake Mead, Nevada/Arizona 46

Lake Michigan, Mich./Ind./Wisc./Ill. 102

Lake Oahe, South Dakota 24

Lake of the Woods, Minnesota 118

Lake Okeechobee, Florida 64

Lake Ontario, New York 40

Lake Ouachita, Arkansas 32

Lake Powell, Utah/Arizona 86

Lake Sam Rayburn, Texas 132

Lake Texoma, Oklahoma/Texas 54

Miramichi River, New Brunswick 18

Montauk Point, New York 70

Niagara River, New York 30

Nova Scotia 112

Nueltin Lake, Manitoba 26

Ottawa River, Ontario 113

Red River, Manitoba 44

Rivers Inlet, British Columbia 48

Sea of Cortez, Mexico 122

St. Lawrence River, New York 78

San Diego, California 92

Santee-Cooper, South Carolina 126

Southwestern New Brunswick 130

Squam Lake, New Hampshire 110

Toledo Bend Reservoir, Texas 36

Truman Lake, Missouri 10

Victoria Island, Northwest Territories 134

Walker's Cay, Bahamas 24

West Point Lake, Georgia 140

White River, Arkansas 6

PHOTO CREDITS 142

ACKNOWLEDGMENTS 142

CONTACT INFORMATION 142

1. **Alagnak River**, Alaska
2. **Ashuanipi River**, Labrador
3. **Atlin**, British Columbia
4. **Attawapiskat River**, Ontario
5. **Beaverkill River**, New York
6. **Bermuda**
7. **Big Sand Lake**, Manitoba
8. **Boundary Waters Canoe Area**, Minnesota
9. **Broadback River**, Quebec
10. **Cabo San Lucas**, Mexico
11. **Campbell River**, British Columbia
12. **Chantrey Inlet**, Northwest Territories
13. **Columbia River**, Oregon/Washington
14. **Cozumel**, Mexico
15. **Delaware River**, New York/Pennsylvania
16. **English River**, Labrador
17. **Florida Keys**, Florida
18. **French River**, Ontario
19. **Gouin Reservoir**, Quebec
20. **Great Bear Lake**, Northwest Territories
21. **Great Slave Lake**, Northwest Territories
22. **Greer's Ferry Lake**, Arkansas
23. **Kawartha Lakes**, Ontario
24. **Kentucky and Barkley Lakes**, Ky./Tenn.
25. **Kepimits Lake**, Labrador
26. **Lac Beauchene**, Quebec
27. **Lake Erie**, Ohio/Pennsylvania
28. **Lake Eufaula**, Alabama/Georgia
29. **Lake Guntersville**, Alabama
30. **Lake Kissimmee**, Florida
31. **Lake Mead**, Nevada/Arizona
32. **Lake Michigan**, Mich./Ind./Wisc./Ill.
33. **Lake Oahe**, South Dakota
34. **Lake of the Woods**, Minnesota
35. **Lake Okeechobee**, Florida
36. **Lake Ontario**, New York
37. **Lake Ouachita**, Arkansas
38. **Lake Powell**, Utah/Arizona
39. **Lake Sam Rayburn**, Texas
40. **Lake Texoma**, Oklahoma/Texas
41. **Miramichi River**, New Brunswick
42. **Montauk Point**, New York
43. **Niagara River**, New York
44. **Nova Scotia**
45. **Nueltin Lake**, Manitoba
46. **Ottawa River**, Ontario
47. **Red River**, Manitoba
48. **Rivers Inlet**, British Columbia
49. **Sea of Cortez**, Mexico
50. **St. Lawrence River**, New York
51. **San Diego**, California
52. **Santee-Cooper**, South Carolina
53. **Southwestern New Brunswick**
54. **Squam Lake**, New Hampshire
55. **Toledo Bend Reservoir**, Texas
56. **Truman Lake**, Missouri
57. **Victoria Island**, Northwest Territories
58. **Walker's Cay**, Bahamas
59. **West Point Lake**, Georgia
60. **White River**, Arkansas

4

FOREWORD

Having fished on five continents, I can say without reservation that no continent matches North America for diversity and quality of sport fisheries. None come even close, in fact.

North America is blessed with great, almost-great, and just-plain-good angling from ocean to gulf, river to lake, highlands to lowlands, region to region. This fishing is, remarkably, publicly accessible with few exceptions, although some of its best waters are difficult, and relatively expensive, to reach because of their remoteness.

The task of selecting the sixty sites to be included in this book, therefore, was not easy. It was arbitrary, to be sure—since there are many highly notable locales that are not detailed—but certainly not capricious, as these sixty were culled from an original list that would have doubled or tripled the size of this book.

In selecting these sites, I tried to take many things into consideration, not the least of which was getting a fair representation of different types of waters, species of gamefish, and regional coverage for readers of all persuasions and interests. The text and the range of photographs reflect these considerations.

Thus, prime saltwater fishing is represented in Mexico, Canada, the United States, Bermuda, and the Bahamas (which technically are not part of North America, but are in a practical sense). The most prominent freshwater gamefish—including bass, muskellunge, walleyes, steelhead, trout, and salmon—are represented in diverse locales throughout the book. Also, there are waters included in this book that can be accessed practically from well-traveled interstate highways and others that can only be reached via float-plane dropoff into the bush country.

For the most part, big bodies of water and/or large areas are profiled here; most are relatively easy to find on a map. Big waters are not the only ones that deserve to be called "great," but they are most capable of producing the size and volume of sportfish consistent with high-quality angling for numerous fishermen.

Because North America is such a large continent, it is hard to fairly represent all areas; nevertheless, locales range from Mexico to the Arctic and the Pacific Northwest to Florida. Many, although less than half, of the locales are Canadian, which bears some commentary. Canada is a vast country with prodigious waterways and such abundant and desirable angling that tens of thousands of visiting anglers sample its bounty each season.

So, whether you desire to cast a fly to brook trout, troll a strip bait for sailfish, toss a surface plug for largemouth bass, bounce a wobbler to salmon, or try your hand at any of the other great sportfishing activities on this continent, you'll find the best places to do it in GREATEST FISHING LOCALES OF NORTH AMERICA.

Ken Schultz

THE **WHITE RIVER** IS LOCATED IN NORTH-CENTRAL ARKANSAS, FLOWING OUT OF BULL SHOALS AND NORFOLK LAKES NEAR MOUNTAIN HOME.

The cold, dam-released water of the White River creates a fog on most summer mornings, causing early-rising boaters to proceed cautiously. These long, shallow-draft johnboats are the typical fishing vessel of the White.

WHITE RIVER
Arkansas

The White River is something of an anomaly. At certain times, such as when the water is high, it does not look like much of a trout stream. When the water is low, and you can see every submerged boulder and pebble from a long distance, a fisherman cannot help but wonder how it is conceivable for huge trout to dwell in it and not have escaped capture long before reaching gargantuan proportions. And in the short-sleeve-shirt heat of a typical mid-South summer day, one marvels at the fact that the river is densely shrouded in fog every morning and that a light jacket is needed to ward off the chill.

But the White River, once a free-flowing smallmouth bass stream, is indeed magna-cum-laude trout water, although not in the sense of a Rocky Mountain river. That's because it is the perpetually cold-water outflow of Bull Shoals and Norfolk lakes. Its level is largely regulated by the amount of water being released from those reservoirs, which varies according to time of year, weather, and so forth.

It is, without question, the most prolific producer of big, actually *huge*, brown trout in North America. The White River and its 4-mile-long tributary, the North Fork, annually produce one or more brown trout in the 20- to 30-pound range. Several browns over 30 pounds have been caught here, including the unofficial all-time world record of 38 pounds, 9 ounces (not recognized as a record because a treble hook was used with bait), as well as four existing line-class world records, including one each of 33 and 34 pounds.

Perhaps ninety percent of the trout caught here are not browns, however, but rainbows, and most of these are very small, befitting what is primarily a hatchery-supported fishery. Cutthroat trout exist, too. Some rainbows of larger size

are caught, but the browns of all sizes are generally wary and more selective. Nonetheless, most of the biggest browns succumb to a bait offering, sometimes one that involves the use of marshmallows, cheese, or salmon eggs. Bait, including worms and crickets, is by far the favorite local offering. Fishing with artificials, including small spinners and flies, is less popular but certainly productive. Light lines and tippets, however, are necessary because of the clarity of the water.

Most of the fishing is done by anglers anchored or drifting their lines from 20-foot-long, flat-bottomed johnboats equipped with small outboard motors on a raised transom in order to get through the shallow riffles. Some anglers wade. The best fishing is usually in the upper reaches: in the North Fork River below the dam to its confluence with the White River, and on the White River from the dam down to the town of Cotter. It is a year-round fishery.

It hardly seems possible that such clear and shallow water could produce so many monster brown trout. Drifting with bait, as these anglers are doing, is the primary fishing method.

THE BULK OF **LAKE ERIE**, INCLUDING THE MOST ATTRACTIVE SHALLOW WESTERN BASIN AND ISLANDS, IS LOCATED IN OHIO.

From a lake with a former reputation for no fish and plenty of pollution to a lake with a reputation as one of the best in the country, Erie has made a truly remarkable turnabout.

LAKE ERIE
Ohio/Pennsylvania

All of the Great Lakes have some good bass and/or good walleye fishing, but none can top that of Lake Erie, which is the second smallest of the five and the shallowest, with an average depth over its 9,900 surface acres of only 62 feet. The western basin in particular, all of which is in Ohio, is blessed with a generally shallow (35 feet and less) environment and a lot of typical smallmouth and walleye habitat—rocky islands and reefs.

Erie especially hosts a phenomenal population of walleyes, including an extraordinary number of fish in the 8-pound-and-over class, some even up to 13 pounds. Crankbaits and spinner-with-worm rigs account for most of the fish in trolling presentations. Good walleye angling can be had in the western basin, which bills itself as the "walleye capital of the world," including the islands region, and eastward through Pennsylvania to Dunkirk, New York. That's a lot of water to cover, but plenty of big walleyes make it well worth the while. Trolling with sideplaners and downriggers using spoons and plugs has become a hot walleye fishing method in Lake Erie over the past few years, primarily because of the abundance of suspended fish. The walleyes suspend themselves over deeper water to take advantage of the roving schools of bait at those levels.

Bass, however, do not suspend as such, but some of these fish, too, are quite large. The western basin islands and also the easterly waters in Ohio and Pennsylvania are producing bronzebacks in the 5-pound range. Anglers are both trolling and casting for these fish through the season, using crankbaits, spinner-and-nightcrawler rigs, and jigs.

The most prominent bass fishery in the western region centers on the aptly named Bass Islands. The points around all three Bass Islands offer good places to start your fishing activities, and the nearby islands of Rattlesnake, Green, Sugar, Kelleys, and Ballast have merit, too.

Lake Erie is a big body of water, and one that can get rough

in a hurry, but this is not scaring off legions of fishermen, including some who are judiciously using very small boats. That's because both smallmouths and walleyes are plentiful, so plentiful, in fact, that the charter-boat skippers consider it a bad day if everyone doesn't catch several fish.

A prodigious population of walleyes is the foremost attraction to sportfishermen. This angler holds a walleye that would be large for most lakes, but is of average size for Lake Erie.

HARRY S. TRUMAN RESERVOIR IS LOCATED IN AN AREA OF THE OZARKS KNOWN FOR ITS IMPOUNDMENTS AND FISHING OPPORTUNITIES. A SHORT DISTANCE FROM SPRINGFIELD, IT IS ACCESSED PRIMARILY FROM THE WARSAW AREA.

The challenges for sportsmen on Truman Lake include navigating boats through the dense flooded timber, finding fish in places that all look so attractive, and then wrestling with the fish they do catch to get them out of the cover.

TRUMAN LAKE
Missouri

Some call Truman Lake in Missouri the "best largemouth lake in North America." There is little doubt that this lake is one of the best for sure and has contributed to the bass fishing boom.

The lake—officially known as Harry S. Truman Reservoir—is yet young as bass lakes go. In 1979 the Corps of Engineers finished building a dam at Warsaw that created a body of water with a normal pool containment of 55,000 acres. Most newly created impoundments go through a fishing boom period before stabilizing, and no doubt this partially explains why the bass population has been so strong here.

However, bass existing in farm ponds before the lake was impounded provided the nucleus of a healthy population. Bass up to 14 pounds have been caught here, and this lake's fish are pot-bellied, owing to an excellent shad forage base. Truman's largemouths have had a faster growth rate than bass in other Missouri impoundments.

Truman features four arms, formed by the Osage, Pomme de Terre, and Grand rivers, as well as by Tebo Creek. Each arm snakes through south-central Missouri woods that bridge Ozark hills to the south and flatlands to the north. Coves, sloughs, embayments, and river and creek feeders are plentiful. While you may have in excess of a 50-mile boat ride from the dam to the farthest points of any of the arms, all the little nooks and crannies contribute to a total of 958 miles of shoreline. Thus, literally hundreds of potentially productive fishing grounds lie along these arms, and it takes a lot of fishing to narrow down the places that yield fish at a given time of the year.

Moreover, in addition to varied layout and topography, Truman is blessed with more bass cover than any one lake deserves. More than half of this lake is heavily timbered. When this lake was created, most of the dogwood, sycamore, and

Muddy, turbid water is characteristic of Truman, particularly in the spring, so fishing close to the trees and using spinner-baits, as this angler has done, are prime tactics for catching largemouth bass.

Big, healthy largemouths are the main quarry for most anglers. Flipping, or using plastic worms or jigs dropped around timber clumps, is a productive, seasonlong technique.

cedar trees, plus all the brush and bushes, were left intact. That makes for an awful lot of bassy-looking cover in which to fish, some tricky moments in navigation and boat handling, and interesting presentations.

If you are used to fishing vegetation, deep lakes, clear lakes, or treeless, coverless lakes, Truman is an entirely different ballgame. It has predominantly muddy or stained water color and an average depth of 15 feet, meaning that bass are relatively shallow all year long. Though it doesn't have vegetation, there is enough cover to hone your casting skills to a fine point.

In fact, you must be an accurate caster to really be effective at Truman. The bass are regularly found holding very tightly to cover, and they won't venture far to pursue a lure. You don't have to make long casts, however. Such casts are disadvantageous because of the difficulty in controlling a spirited fish through dense timber on a long line. Most casting is at distances ranging from 15 to 30 feet, and you still have to watch the trajectory of the lure and be aware of the interference of overhanging limbs.

For these shallow, timber-dwelling largemouths, the spinnerbait reigns supreme, particularly in the spring. You can catch bass on spinnerbaits in the summer, too, but in the spring the fish are a bit shallower—especially in April when preparing to spawn and moving onto the banks—and they seem to be more aggressive. A black jig, flipped or pitched, is another very strong lure here, and flipping is one of the primary techniques in all seasons, especially summer. Plastic worms account for fish, too, as do crankbaits.

In general, the edges of creek channels are places where bass congregate, as are breaks and points in the timber, old ditches and sloughs, the backs of creeks, and various coves. In the summer, cedar tree rows, trees with brush around them, standing timber in coves with 10 to 15 feet of water, and shoals are productive.

Although bass get most of the glamour and attention here, Truman is also a terrific crappie lake, and serious log and timber fishing for them with jigs and minnows takes places in the spring. The walleye fishery is also picking up and one day may be particularly worthwhile. Striped bass (stripers) and catfish round out the other possibilities.

If you visit Truman to fish for bass, think of it as a challenge. It's a challenge to navigate; find fish; catch fish; keep your balance when the boat hits a tree while the electric motor is in use; retrieve your lures properly; cast accurately; keep your line in good condition; unsnag your lures successfully time after time; and, of course, muscle those heavy-bellied largemouths through the woods.

In addition to bass, Truman has a great population of crappies and an emerging walleye fishery.

13

CAMPBELL RIVER
British Columbia

The great migrations of Pacific salmon include fish heading north and south, all destined ultimately to ascend rivers of the Pacific Northwest. During their migration, they encounter Vancouver Island, and a great body of fish pass to the eastern side of that island, which eventually takes them through the Discovery Passage, funneling through Campbell River, a Canadian island town that has long billed itself, with some merit, as the "salmon capital of the world."

Check this locale out when the runs are on and the action is fast, and you will not dispute the claim. In fact, you'll find it hard to count the number of boats, literally several thousand, within a few miles of Campbell River itself. No, this is not virgin country fishing, but it has been, and still is, among the best, and a mecca for salmon and steelhead anglers.

There are intricate tidal currents here, and the best king (chinook) salmon fishing is in such locales as the gigantic back eddy in front of the lighthouse where the Strait of Georgia and Discovery Passage meet, and in Seymour Nar-

CAMPBELL RIVER IS ONE HOUR FROM VANCOUVER AND IS ACCESSED BY FLOAT PLANE (WITH WATER-TAXI SERVICE) OR WHEELED AIRCRAFT FROM THE MAINLAND. ANGLERS WITH BOAT IN TOW CAN FERRY TO VICTORIA AND DRIVE NORTH.

A 35-pound king salmon, earning the Indian name tyee, is cause for smiles from angler and guide alike. This one was taken at the famous Lighthouse Pool.

Bathed in early morning light, members of the Tyee Club practice a century-old sporting tradition, rowing for salmon out of old skiffs near the Campbell River.

rows—where, on an especially high tide, the current can flow as great as 16 knots, and there may be 50- to 60-foot-wide whirlpools. Several kings of 60 pounds are caught here every season, though it is more likely to get them one-third that size.

The major lodges, especially April Point, which is the largest and arguably the best, place a lot of emphasis on sportsmanship, so there is a good deal of fishing done with relatively light tackle. It is popular to use light line, long rods, and fly reels to fish for coho salmon, so a scrappy bout is virtually ensured. Mooching with herring is the main method of salmon fishing, even with light gear, and some angling is done here with artificials, with trolling and jigging practiced.

Rowing from skiffs is still done by members of the Tyee Club and their guests at sunrise and sunset.

There is, incidentally, also some fall and winter river fishing for sea-run cutthroat trout and for steelhead. The area can be fished all year long, no matter what direction the wind may be from, so you can plan a trip well in advance with an assurance of meeting fishable conditions.

For big king salmon, plan on August; for big cohos, September and October. June is excellent for general action, with May also a good bet because there are fewer grilse (young salmon on their first return from the sea) around. Generally, coho average 5 to 6 pounds, with bigger (referred to here as "northern") coho in the 6- to 12-pound range in the fall.

With a scenic coast for background, anglers drift their cut-herring baits through Seymour Narrows, one of the swiftest sections of water in the area.

LAKE GUNTERSVILLE
Alabama

LOCATED IN NORTH-
EASTERN ALABAMA,
LAKE GUNTERSVILLE
IS A NARROW, LONG
IMPOUNDMENT ON
THE TENNESSEE RIVER.

Some folks call Lake Guntersville "the best bass lake in Alabama," and while that is a debatable point in a state with several topnotch largemouth waters, it does put this impoundment on the Tennessee River in very high company.

It is definitely the largest impoundment in that state, and its 69,000 acres—including many creeks, islands, and flats—are loaded with plenty of big bass. Guntersville is also rife with water milfoil and hydrilla vegetation, which has been to some degree responsible for the good fishery, but is the source of some concern in the future. Estimates range from

Summer in Alabama is hot, and most anglers fish early and late in the day and at night, but good results can be had all season long.

twenty to forty percent in assessing the amount of this lake that is covered with vegetation, and steps to eradicate or control it are being hotly debated. For the present, at least, the situation is quite favorable for largemouth bass anglers.

Obviously, bass fishing revolves around the vegetation to some degree virtually all season long, and weedless lures and surface lures are of great value. Surface fishing with floating plugs, buzz baits, and plastic frogs or mice (called "rats" here) provides good sport, and success comes with spinnerbaits and plastic worms. Worms, rigged Texas-style and pegged so the slip sinker doesn't hang on the vegetation, are the foremost lure for thick vegetation, especially in warm weather and on bright days. Flipping worms into the openings of the matted vegetation is effective here. When fish are aggressive and early in the season before the grass has grown up fully, shallow-running crankbaits and lipless crankbaits have merit.

With the exception of the winter, there is no poor bass fishing time. Spring means spawning activity from mid-March into May, and fall brings good surface fishing. Thanks to the vegetation, summer fishing can be highly productive for the good worm angler.

Most anglers direct their efforts toward fishing the vegetation that is closest to the main river channel, and sometimes that is all that is necessary. But milfoil and hydrilla beds situated well back in creeks or bays can be very productive, too. Roseberry Creek, which is in the vicinity of Scottsboro, and Browns Creek, below the town of Guntersville, are two of the best choices.

A late-fall angler swings a nice bass into the boat. Visible on the far right is the line of vegetation that attracts such fish on Lake Guntersville.

THE MAIN SOUTHWEST **MIRAMICHI** IS LOCATED IN EAST-CENTRAL NEW BRUNSWICK, WITH DOAKTOWN BEING THE HUB OF INFORMATION AND ACTIVITY.

MIRAMICHI RIVER
New Brunswick

In some circles the king of gamefish is none other than the Atlantic salmon, and when one thinks of places to fish for this hallowed species, the Canadian province of New Brunswick comes immediately to mind. Atlantic salmon ascend more than fifty of this province's rivers, with about fifteen having significant runs. Of these, none hosts more salmon and grilse, nor is more renowned, than the fabled Miramichi.

The Main Southwest Miramichi is the focal point for intense salmon angling efforts from July through September annually, and despite the well-chronicled troubles of salmon in the modern era, the runs here and throughout this province have been getting stronger in each of the last few years, with larger fish (though not at historical levels) also becoming more available.

In a common Miramichi scene, these salmon anglers have taken a midday, prelunch respite to milk in the lodge ambience. This image was captured at Old River Lodge, Doaktown.

Long outboard-powered canoes are a familiar sight, both for transportation and fishing, on the Miramichi. Late evening, when this action was captured, is prime for salmon throughout the season and for shad in the spring.

The large fish cannot be kept, which has been one of several principal contributing factors in this resurgence. In fact, you cannot keep a salmon that is larger than 63 centimeters, or 25 inches, under any circumstance, which effectively limits the take (ten fish per season) to grilse anyway.

All Atlantic salmon fishing here by law is fly-fishing with an unweighted artificial fly. Most of this is dry fly-fishing, using large deer-hair flies, many brightly colored, on 9-foot rods with 8 or 9 weight lines, although wet flies on floating lines are also employed.

The Main Southwest Miramichi is a lovely, long, winding, generally shallow, river with many bars and pools, and it is an easy river to wade under most circumstances. It is wide by the standards of most trout fishermen, and its regular anglers are known for long casting, although that is not an absolute necessity.

Fishing in early September, the author makes a typical downstream presentation for Atlantic salmon. Angling on the Miramichi is restricted to fly-fishing, and although it is not always necessary, long casts are the norm.

The fishing season varies from river to river in New Brunswick, but, by way of example, the Miramichi opened in 1989 on June 8 for bright (fresh-run) salmon and closed on October 7, the closing being a little later than it has been in past years.

June fishing is often spotty, with July being the time when there is usually a good number of fish available. September has produced excellent angling in recent years, although there is often some fluctuation in availability of fish and the occurrence of fresh runs due to water levels, rainfall, and the warmth (or coolness) of the weather in a given year.

The major pools on this river (and on many others) are in private hands, being leased or owned predominantly by clubs or sporting camps, and one cannot simply walk to the river and take a rod out and start angling anywhere, although there is some public water. Nonresident anglers must have a licensed guide everywhere on this river, as well as on other New Brunswick waters that are "designated."

In addition to the bright salmon fishing, the Miramichi has excellent sport for so-called black salmon—those returning to sea after wintering in the river—and these fish are readily caught on the fly, providing an especially good introduction to Atlantic salmon fishing for the angler who is new to the species and/or to fly-fishing. This is an overlooked opportunity on the Miramichi, albeit one that is not preferred by some salmon traditionalists.

The Miramichi also hosts an excellent run of American shad in late May/early June. This, too, is virtually neglected. As with salmon, shad angling is done by fly-fishing with unweighted flies only, primarily by casting from anchored canoes. The fish run from 2.5 to 5 pounds on average, but much larger ones are present, and the possibility exists for establishing a tippet-class fly-rod record if one is diligent and lucky. When the run is strong, an angler can get into some very fast action with these fish.

Noted New Brunswick fisherman Bill Ensor displays a typical Miramichi grilse.

BEAVERKILL RIVER
New York

There is probably no other trout river in North America that is known as widely within the continent, and outside of it, as New York's Beaverkill. There is no other river that has been as widely written about, and which has been so detailed in trout and fly-fishing literature, as this body of water.

The Beaverkill is a relatively modest body of water in general terms, flowing for some 45 miles to its confluence with the east branch of the Delaware River. The upper half is almost entirely private. From Roscoe, which is billed as "Trout Town U.S.A.," the Beaverkill is joined by the Willowemoc River at famous Junction Pool, becoming a larger river, and the remaining 20-mile length is open to public fishing. This includes a lot of renowned "no-kill" water, which produces excellent catch-and-release fishing with artificial lures only all season long, and especially when major fly hatches occur. The two stretches of water with these special regulations provide the best angling.

Brown trout are the primary catch, although an occasional rainbow is taken. Dry flies are the preference of most anglers here, especially as the many well-known pools of the Beaverkill are hallowed dry-fly water, and there is barely a time when the major pools do not have some fishermen, many from faraway locales, giving them a fling.

THE **BEAVERKILL RIVER** IS LOCATED IN THE SOUTH-WESTERN SECTION OF THE CATSKILL MOUNTAINS.

Anglers work Barnhart's Pool on the Beaverkill, a noted spot and part of the highly successful and popular no-kill waters on this river.

SITUATED IN SOUTH-
CENTRAL FLORIDA, LAKE
KISSIMMEE IS ONE OF
TWENTY CONNECTED
LAKES ON THE
KISSIMMEE RIVER.

*This is the type of fish that
draws many thousands of
anglers a year to Florida
and to Lake Kissimmee.
Trophy-size largemouth bass
are primarily caught on
wild shiners, although this
beauty fell to a plastic worm.*

LAKE KISSIMMEE
Florida

Very few people from outside of Florida properly pronounce the name of this lake (it sounds like "kiss-him-me" said quickly, not "kiss-a-me"), but they have little trouble explaining what draws them to this big waterway: outsize largemouth bass. In a state with a lot of places that produce lunkers, this lake is definitely one of the shining stars.

In its history, Lake Kissimmee has reputedly yielded two bass over 16 pounds, and a plethora of fish over the magic and pot-bellied size of 10 pounds. Many of the big bass don't see a fisherman for long periods of time, as this lake has far more cows grazing along its shoreline than it ever does anglers casting to its endless vegetation.

The fact that Lake Kissimmee is not really close to a major population center and that there are a lot of good bass fishing opportunities in south-central Florida (including nearby lakes like Tohopekaliga and Hatchineha) contributes to this. So does the nature of the lake. It is 8.5 miles wide at its greatest point and shallow, meaning that when a storm or wind kicks up it gets dangerous very quickly, so knowledgeable anglers give it a lot of respect.

Lake Kissimmee is loaded with vegetation, including hayfields and lily pads, and if there is a dilemma it is where to actually concentrate your efforts when so much of the lake looks good. Compared to some places, that is a rather enviable problem. The islands of Storm, Lemon, Bird, Brahma, and Grassy as well as Philadelphia Point are well-known spots, but they require some study and serious working to get to know. Facing 46,000 acres of good-looking, heavily vegetated cover, average visitors have their work cut out for them without a guide. But, of course, the reward potential is

significant.

Most of the big largemouths are taken by fishing with large, wild shiners. This is a well-known Florida big-bass ploy, and the shiners, some as large as 10 inches, are fished on bobbers or free-lined, usually worked in deep holes or on the edges of dense cover.

Lures work, too, and you can pin your best hopes on a large plastic worm, which is the other big-bass staple here. Weedless spoons and spinnerbaits catch some fish, as well as surface lures, but shiners and plastic worms are the hands-down favorites if big bass are the quarry.

Most big largemouths are caught here in the winter, but that is because there is far more angling activity then. Cold fronts can put a whammy on bass during the winter, so be forewarned. The summer is greatly overlooked, with little pressure and good opportunities to catch big bass, especially early in the day.

Lake Kissimmee and the other lakes on the chain have been good to anglers who are adept at working vegetative cover.

WALKER'S CAY
Bahamas

In World War II, it was an antisubmarine base. In 1990, it hosted several dozen professional athletes for a world fishing championship tournament that was broadcast on ESPN.

Yes, Walker's Cay, the northernmost island in the Bahamas, has had a diverse existence.

Today it is known as a premier sportfishing locale. Here, where numerous world records have been established, and its fishing opportunities are as diverse as its past.

The offshore fishing and reef-bottom fishing are especially acclaimed. There is simply no better place in the Bahamas for reef fishing, and this is an all-season opportunity. Here, the coral drops off just a short distance away, and this provides action for various species of grouper. The larger ones—plus the occasional African pompano, shark, amberjack, barracuda, and wahoo—are usually taken in 130 to 200 feet of water. Jigging is the principal technique, using stout tackle to keep big fish from getting back into the bottom and an inevitable cutoff.

Walker's principal reputation is for big game. It hosts several major tournaments annually. Most of this activity occurs from late winter through early summer, and blue marlin are the main interest. A deep dropoff nearby and upwelling of bait contribute to this.

The island record for blue marlin is just under 700 pounds. Fish in the 500- and 600-pound class are caught, but the average blue remains under 200. High-speed trolling with lures is preferred, using this as a way to cover a lot of territory, and the best fishing usually takes place from February through May. March and April are considered prime here for blue marlin, but these fish may be encountered through the year.

LEADING THE ABACO CHAIN AND THE NORTHERNMOST ISLAND IN THE BAHAMAS, **WALKER'S CAY** IS 150 MILES NORTHEAST OF FORT LAUDERDALE, FLORIDA, AND 110 MILES EAST OF PALM BEACH.

Several center-console boats leave the harbor at Walker's Cay, bound for the nearby reef or blue water. Being close to Florida, this island is especially popular with owners of small- to medium-size craft.

Other fish that are fairly common through the entire season are wahoo, mackerel, and blackfin tuna. Dolphin action is sporadic, but the fish are fairly large. White marlin are mainly caught during the winter and spring. Sailfish are most abundant in summer and fall. Yellowfin tuna are a summer catch.

Incidentally, while Walker's Cay is not on a par other locales where bonefish can be caught, the action for this species is nonetheless pretty good and makes an interesting diversion from reef and offshore angling.

Walker's Cay is frequently visited by anglers boating across the Gulf Stream from south Florida, which is about a four-hour journey in relatively calm seas. Flats anglers fish nearby, jiggers fish the inshore reefs and offshore north and west at Mantanilla Reef (although this is 40 miles away), while bluewater trollers work the edge of the dropoff. An easterly current, and a quick dropoff from the Abaco wall to 100-fathom-deep water and more, means that Walker's Cay is a fifteen-minute run from harbor to productive big game grounds.

A small blue marlin is about to be released to Bahamian waters. Billfish tournaments are a popular mainstay at Walker's.

NUELTIN LAKE, WHICH STRADDLES THE SIXTIETH PARALLEL, IS ABOUT 850 MILES NORTH OF WINNIPEG. IT IS ACCESSED FROM WINNIPEG AND THOMPSON BY A TURBO-PROP PLANE THAT LANDS AT A PRIVATE AIRSTRIP AT TREELINE LODGE.

A monster lake trout like this is cause for smiles and photographs and is precisely the kind of fish that draws anglers to the most remote reaches of Manitoba. On Nueltin, even such trophies as this are released.

NUELTIN LAKE
Manitoba

Nueltin Lake is a place where a freshwater fisherman's dreams of plenty can truly be realized. Lots of trout and pike, even fish of enormous size, are an honest-to-goodness possibility for any visitor who is even a moderately skilled angler. This is a rather remarkable thing to say in the modern era of overfished places, but having been to Nueltin recently, and having had my own lake trout fishing experience of a lifetime, I say it with full conviction.

Nueltin Lake's awesome fishing history is still being written because the angling is getting even better. The reason: It's a catch-and-release lake. This policy is adhered to as strictly by the Gurke family, who own the only accommodations on this 125-mile-long lake, as it was by the previous owners, who originated it. There are no heavily laden fish

boxes leaving Treeline Lodge, which is the Gurkes' main facility, or their outpost camps at Windy River and Nueltin Narrows. Such fish as 20-pound pike and 40-pound lakers go back into the water, as do 5- and 15-pounders. Only one fish under 10 pounds can be kept for shore lunch, and any large fish that dies becomes the property of the camp.

Some day, there may be a problem with this policy when a guest catches a new all-tackle world-record lake trout (the present all-tackle world record is 65 pounds, and the lodge best is 56) and wants to take it home. Such a fish could be kept, but the Gurkes offer a five-thousand-dollar stipend to the guest that lands and releases it alive.

How will they know its weight? Camp boats have a length-girth-weight chart laminated to the inside gunwale and are supplied with a measuring tape. Anglers take the length and girth measurements and a quick photo, release their fish, then consult with the chart to determine the weight. The fish, which are predominantly caught in relatively shallow water, are released unharmed, provided anglers handle them carefully and are quick to get them back in the cool water, holding them upright and by the tail for a moment to ensure their stability.

Since a trophy-only policy was begun in 1977, and subsequently changed to a complete catch-and-release policy, there has been a steady increase in the number of trophy fish (20 pounds merits official trophy status for Manitoba pike and lake trout) caught and released at Nueltin. Using barbless, single-hooked lures, incidentally, is another lodge policy, and a necessary one because of the need to release fish unharmed and because of the amount of action encountered,

not to mention the safety factor in unhooking fish, especially pike.

Nueltin fishing lends itself to various angling techniques. For big lake trout, trolling is undoubtedly the best tactic, especially in the main part of the lake. However, early in the season, when the ice is still receding, the bays and river inlets with open water offer the best chances for huge fish, with possibilities for light-tackle angling as well as casting and jigging. Spoons and large jigs are the best lures, and DeBartok Rapids and Sealhole Lake are two prime locales.

For pike, the period of mid-June (when the camps open) through early July probably offers the most action, with plenty of fish in shallow water that are eager to strike surface

Just you, a fishing rod, and miles of virtually virgin water is a typical scenario for fishermen at Nueltin Lake. This image was taken at Windy River, a locale found about midlake.

A young angler casts his lure into remote and seldom fished Sealhole Lake, into which Nueltin empties at its northern end. One cast here could produce the trout of a lifetime.

lures, spinnerbaits, and weedless spoons that are cast into the shore in the backs of countless bays. Good pike and lake trout fishing can be had through the entire, thirteen-week season, which lasts from mid-June until the first week of September.

Nueltin, incidentally, also offers grayling fishing. Some good-size fish, in the 3-pound-range, are caught here, especially by anglers fishing the swifter water around Nueltin Narrows.

Although known mostly for lakers, Nueltin Lake has some extraordinary northern pike fishing. This 20-pounder was caught in the back of one of Nueltin's countless bays.

The Manitoba Master Angler program is testimony to the lake's great pike and lake trout fishing, and if it wasn't for the fact that two-thirds of Nueltin lies in the Northwest Territories and trophy fish caught in those waters aren't registered in this government program, Nueltin would dominate the stat sheet far more than it does presently.

Fishermen who go to Nueltin, however, don't need statistics or other numbers to tell them that this is a quality place. It is, of course, as remote as one can get in Manitoba, with wild, unspoiled beauty, countless islands and bays, many incoming rivers, and plenty of sandy beaches where you might see the tracks of a moose, wolf, or bear—if not the animal itself. The southern portion is amply treed with spruce and tamarack, and the terrain tapers to stark tundra at the northern end, where caribou are occasionally seen.

The trouble with Nueltin Lake is that it may be *too* good. When you get into nonstop pike action, for example, with all the boils and swirls and splashes and other excitement, you might become jaded. How do you follow that act? When you hook a bunch of trophy lake trout and see still bigger fish swim away, what could realistically be an encore?

I've concluded that there are just two solutions. The first is to never leave. Famous trapper Ragner Jonsson lived on fish and game for thirty-eight years at Nueltin, until he died in 1988 at age eighty-eight. He had tepees scattered over this vast lake and told lodge employees of great fish in many places, some of which remain unexplored by visiting anglers to this day.

The other solution is less harsh: Keep coming back.

Angling at the treacherous Devil's Hole on the lower Niagara River, a fisherman struggles to overcome a powerful fish that is headed downriver and toward the swift water that passes through the turbulent discharge of the Niagara-Mohawk power station.

CLOSEST TO BUFFALO, AND FORMING A BOUNDARY BETWEEN ONTARIO AND NEW YORK, THE MIGHTY **NIAGARA RIVER** IS THE LINK BETWEEN LAKE ONTARIO AND THE REST OF THE GREAT LAKES WATERSHED.

NIAGARA RIVER
New York

There are certainly some impressive things about New York State's Niagara River. There is, of course, *the* falls. Niagara, derived from the Indian word *ongiara*, meaning "thundering water," is certainly an appropriate name for this wonder, which inspires awe in everyone who watches the Great Lakes flush there amid a tumultuous spray arched by a rainbow.

Efforts to harness hydroelectric energy from it are impressive. The Niagara Power Project, located a short distance below the falls, is one of the world's largest hydroelectric-power-producing facilities. And then there are the *Maid of the Mist* boat rides, the Cave of the Catacombs walk, the wax museum, and the other attractions and treasures that contribute to making this locale one of the favorite honeymoon destinations of North America.

To a fisherman, however, the Niagara River holds another type of treasure: some of the best and most varied of all angling on the Great Lakes and its tributaries.

Those treasures most notably include perhaps the best run of large salmon—15 to 35 pounds—in the Great Lakes each fall in the Niagara Gorge at Devil's Hole, above which no boats pass and which possesses some of the most treacherous white water in the East. From the falls to miles below past Lewiston, the lower Niagara River is a steep, forbidding gorge. But it yields some awesome fishing to the diligent and careful angler. Drifting with preserved-salmon-egg clusters is most productive for obtaining these fish, but flat-line trolling with deep-diving plugs is a hot second, especially early in the day. Shore casters fish eggs, plugs, and spoons.

From mid-October through April, steelhead are present in the lower Niagara in good number, with best action in February and March; drifting with eggs is the main technique, but other methods are possible, including fly-fishing. The river gets a virtually neglected run of lake trout, incidentally, in May, and angling for this species is surprisingly good. At other times, walleyes, smallmouth bass, and perch fill the bill. There are a lot of smallmouth here, as well as walleyes that top 10 pounds. The upper river (above the falls) is noted for bass, walleyes, perch, and muskies throughout the summer and fall.

No doubt, the idea of sportfishing never occurs to most Niagara Falls visitors, which is just as well if you are a fisherman and can get there to take advantage of it.

A typical chinook salmon on its fall river migration is brought to net. The Niagara River hosts a phenomenal run of large salmon each fall.

LAKE OUACHITA IS ABOUT 35 MILES FROM HOT SPRINGS, REACHED BY TAKING U.S. 270 WEST.

LAKE OUACHITA
Arkansas

One of the toughest things to do in freshwater fishing is stop a runaway striped bass. When that striper weighs over 20 pounds, you've got a battle on your hands; and when that striper has treetops to run around, you have your work cut out for you. In fact, some fishermen have resorted to using 50-pound test line and still can't keep the big fish out of the Ouachita trees. That's some kind of problem to deal with in a freshwater lake!

Lake Ouachita didn't always have stripers. It's one of the many lakes in the United States in which inland stripers were stocked to help control the shad forage base and to provide an extra gamefish that would utilize open-water habitat.

There's a lot of open water in Lake Ouachita, but it's still just a fraction of the amount of acreage that encompasses the Ouachita National Forest surrounding this lake. The Corps of Engineers left a lot of timber standing in this lake when it was flooded, a good deal of which is submerged in relatively deep water near creek channels. Some of those trees come to within 20 feet of the surface. If you have a good sonar device on your boat, you can detect every branch of the tree as well as see a striper sitting near the top waiting for some prey to pass by.

The best striper fishing on Ouachita occurs in spring and fall. Summer is generally slow, due in part to the clear water, though some fish can be caught at first light. In the fall,

Late in the season is prime time for striped bass, which can be caught by casting to schooling fish or by trolling deep and utilizing downriggers, as these fishermen are doing.

Lake Ouachita may be the best lake in North America for catching large stripers. This 26-pounder would make any angler happy.

however, stripers school after baitfish, and fishermen experience the most exciting angling of the year—chasing and casting to breaking fish. This is when surface lures like stickbaits and chuggers provide exciting fishing, and when jigs, jigging spoons, tailspinners, and other lures catch fish out of the schools. Trolling for suspended and deeper fish has merit at this time, too, as long as you use plugs or white jigs for lures.

Lake Ouachita may be one of the premier striper lakes in North America, but it is also no slouch in the black bass department. Largemouths have been plentiful here, and it's a great lake to catch spotted (locally called "Kentucky") bass. A Kentucky the same length as a largemouth is chunkier and fights more determinedly.

THE ASSINICA RESERVE AND **BROADBACK RIVER** ARE LOCATED IN NORTH-CENTRAL QUEBEC, WEST OF LAKE MISTASSINI AND NORTHWEST OF CHIBOUGAMAU.

Situated in a remote and wild area, the Broadback River is known for producing large brook trout. No doubt the difficulty in accessing it has contributed to its status as a premier fishery.

BROADBACK RIVER
Quebec

One all-tackle world record that is likely to never be broken is that of the brook trout: a 14.5-pound monster caught in Ontario in 1916. But if there is ever to be a chance, an angler would find it in either Labrador or Quebec these days. The next-largest brook trout (called "speckled trout" in these provinces) in the record books currently is a 10-pound, 7-ounce fish from the Broadback River in the Assinica Reserve of northern Quebec, which shows just what is possible.

While 10-pounders, even 8- or 6-pounders, aren't a guaran-teed experience there, the likelihood of catching a fish over 4 pounds–which by any standards is a very large brook trout—is particularly good, as is the opportunity for having a very pleasing wilderness experience.

The major waters in this area include the Broadback, Rupert, Omo, and Martin rivers, plus the tributaries of 110-mile-long Lake Mistassini. The watershed holds ample fishing for such other species as pike, walleye, and lake trout, and this is all accessed by fly-in visitation, much of it via canoe camping with portages and a lot of adventurous exploration.

ATTAWAPISKAT RIVER
Ontario

The Attawapiskat is a big river in northern Ontario, yet one that relatively few anglers are familiar with, which is interesting because Ontario is a province that has many fishing opportunities, most of which are quite well known to the avid angler. Perhaps it is the locale that does it, since this river is a long distance away, accessible only by float plane.

It is this remoteness, however, that contributes heavily to its status as a premier pike and walleye fishing destination, as well as the fact that it has not been fished heavily over the years. This writer made one of the first visits to a commercial camp here in the late seventies, just when the river was being opened to sportfishing with lodging accommodations, and the fishing was stupendous.

It is still excellent. Big walleyes and pike (over 7 and 15 pounds, respectively) are the hallmark of this pristine and picturesque river, with many suitable locales for both species. Some of the better fishing takes place in the Pym Island area, which is approximately 150 miles north of Nakina.

Good fishing notwithstanding, the Attawapiskat is an attractive place aesthetically, and it is just what the average angler envisions as a wild and remote Canadian fishing locale.

THE **ATTAWAPISKAT RIVER**, WHICH FLOWS INTO HUDSON BAY, IS ABOUT 75 MILES NORTH OF THE ALBANY RIVER IN NORTHERN ONTARIO.

Big northern pike such as this are a prime attraction on the Attawapiskat River. Most of the big pike are caught in the slower-water hideouts, but this was taken on a bend in the main river.

CABO SAN LUCAS IS LOCATED AT THE TIP OF THE BAJA PENINSULA, WHERE THE SEA OF CORTEZ MERGES WITH THE PACIFIC OCEAN.

In the waters off Cabo, billfish are avidly sought by anglers. Although striped marlin are the main quarry, other species, including sailfish, such as this one, are also taken seasonally.

CABO SAN LUCAS
Mexico

Cabo San Lucas is the striped marlin capital of North America, with these fish being available virtually year-round, sometimes in numbers that permit multiple hookups. In addition to having an abundance of striped marlin, most of which are in the 100- to 200-pound class, the area possesses good fishing for other highly desirable species, so Cabo as well as the entire southern portion of Baja California have long been associated with good angling.

The foremost billfish action in this region is in the deep waters off Cabo San Lucas itself, but east and north from Cabo to La Paz is also extremely productive, especially the midsection, which is known as the East Cape. La Paz is the capital of the state of Baja California Sur and provides good fishing nearby at Isla Partida and Isla Espiritu Santo, and a little farther away at Cerralvo Island. Further south in the East Cape region, Punta Pescadero, Punta Colorado, and Buena Vista are the main fishing sites.

The area hosts other billfish, too, including blue and black marlin and sailfish. Blacks are not common, but some large ones have been caught. Blues are more abundant, in 200- to 300-pound sizes, and they show up from summer though fall. Sailfish are predominantly a summer catch. The summer offers an occasional chance at a swordfish as well.

The big-game techniques here involve trolling and live bait angling, using mackerel to catch fish that have been attracted to a boat and to trolling lures. A lot of time is spent searching for fish by looking for working birds, baitfish breaking water, the splash of a breaking marlin, and the like.

Other fisheries include dolphin, or dorado, which are extremely popular and very abundant; roosterfish, which are also abundant, caught fairly close to shore, and found locally up to 90 pounds or so; and for migratory yellowfin tuna, which are found quite large as well.

An exceptionally good area for diverse fishing is near La Paz at Cerralvo Island, which is the southernmost island in the Sea of Cortez. It supports reef fishing for such species as striped pargo, dog snapper, and cabrilla, with the chance of catching a roosterfish or dorado at the same time. These species can be caught inshore along this entire region. There is also good fishing along the western coast of the Baja Peninsula. There are few villages, fishing boats, or access, however, so this has been relatively untapped except for large sportfishing boats that have ventured down the coast from California. A reported billfish hotspot here is off Magdalena Bay, in the middle of Baja California Sur.

These Mexican fishermen have had a successful day for billfish. Although Cabo's fishing is not as plentiful as in the past, it is still very good, and there are opportunities for various species.

LAKE ONTARIO IS
ACCESSED FROM MANY
PORTS AND LOCALES. THE
MAJOR FISHING AREAS
ARE HENDERSON
HARBOR, PULASKI, AND
OSWEGO IN THE EAST;
OLCOTT AND WILSON IN
THE WEST; AND
ROCHESTER,
IRONDEQUOIT BAY, AND
SODUS IN BETWEEN.

*The Salmon River is one of
the best streams in all of
the Great Lakes for
steelhead, which this
successful angler is
bringing to net. Most
steelhead are caught by
the hardy angler from
November through April.*

Marty Salovin, who once held a line-class world-record coho salmon from Lake Ontario, shows a typical 20-pound fall chinook.

LAKE ONTARIO
New York

Some folks go to New Zealand or Argentina for brown and rainbow trout; others try the Pacific Northwest for salmon; and some visit the Northwest Territories for lake trout. So a place that would offer all of these renowned opportunities and be relatively close to millions of people would be a stupendous treasure indeed.

That place exists. It's Lake Ontario, the easternmost body of water in the Great Lakes. And while it may not have the isolation, shoreside vistas, and wilderness charm of some other great angling locales, it surely has the fishing. That ranges from smallmouth bass to perch to numerous trout species and to both Atlantic and Pacific strains of salmon.

The modern-day Lake Ontario fishery was developed through exten-

sive trout- and salmon-stocking efforts, starting with the introduction of coho and chinook salmon in 1968. Today there is no other Great Lakes locale that can rival Lake Ontario and its tributaries for big chinook salmon. Pick the size of fish that you fancy—20, 30, or more pounds, up to 45—and this water has them. This is in large part due to a tremendous forage base of alewives and smelt. Although that similar forage base has suffered in other lakes, it has remained constant in Lake Ontario, the result being that an angler has an extremely good chance of catching a salmon 20 pounds or better here, especially from late August through September, when the mature fish return to natal tributaries to spawn and die.

Although large chinooks are caught throughout this lake, more seem to be available from spring through midsummer in the western sector, from the sandbar off the mouth of the Niagara River to the Rochester area, with particularly good success out of the ports of Olcott and Wilson. The trolling fishery primarily involves downriggers with various spoon types and colors. Plugs are fished successfully early in the season, along with sideplaning and flat-line trolling. Plugs and spoons do the job in late August and September.

Atlantic salmon are caught here, although not with the regularity of chinooks and cohos. An intensified Atlantic-salmon-stocking program, particularly in the eastern basin around the Black River in Dexter, should soon result in a reliable fishery for these creatures both in the lake and river.

Brown trout, lake trout, and steelhead are very popular and found in large sizes here, with fish over 8 pounds common and some to 20 and even 30 pounds. The best brown trout fishing occurs in the spring, from late March through May, near shore. The fish are seeking warm water then and are accessible to shallow-water trollers and casters. Plugs are preferred early, switching to spoons. In May 1990, a 30-pound, 5-ounce brown caught here set a new lake and state record.

Lake trout are found throughout the waters, with strict management regulations to try to encourage their propagation and the reinstitution of an endemic strain. They have been particularly abundant in the eastern basin, which has the reef, island, and bottom structure that typically attracts these fish. Lake trout fishing is exclusively a trolling proposition, usually fairly deep via downriggers.

Steelhead, meanwhile, are very popular, especially being sought by winter and early spring fishermen in the tributaries. They can be found in the major tributaries, especially the Salmon, Niagara, Black, and Oswego rivers, throughout the winter, with fresh runs of fish occurring at various times and peaking when these fish spawn in April. Drifting with bait, either worms or especially egg sacks, is the most popular technique, although these fish are also caught by back-bouncing plugs and casting flies.

The eastern end of Lake Ontario is known for its smallmouth bass fishing and possesses great numbers of these fish. Bass habitat here is excellent, with plenty of rocky shoals, islands, points, and weed-edged rocks from Stony Point all the way to Cape Vincent. There is also good smallmouth fishing in the Sodus-to-Oswego sector. Despite being close to so many people, it is not as heavily exploited for bass as one might think.

That is partially due to the fact that this is big water, and the lake gets extremely rough when the wind kicks up, as it does often, especially from the northwest. Although there are several hundred charter-boat skippers along the lake, there is a great deal of fishing done by private boaters, and care and precaution is mandatory here.

The first fishing of the season on Lake Ontario usually means brown trout, and plenty of them. This 8-pounder, caught by the author, is a good catch, but well below the sizes that are occasionally registered here.

Early in the morning is a prime time for Lake Ontario fishing throughout the season. This daybreak image was made near Oswego and depicts the Nine Mile Point nuclear power plant, which has a warm-water discharge that attracts fish.

The author holds a nice cat, but one that is not particularly large for the Red River and its tributaries. The fish was caught in Winnipeg on the Assiniboine River, which flows into the Red.

THE **RED RIVER** IS IN THE VICINITY OF LOCKPORT, NOT FAR FROM THE CITY OF WINNIPEG, AND ATTRACTS BOTH WALLEYE AND CATFISH ANGLERS.

RED RIVER
Manitoba

To many anglers a walleye over 4 or 5 pounds is a nice fish, but avid walleye fishermen know that they really have something to brag about if they catch a fish in the 8-pound-and-over class. Walleyes this size are caught in a number of places, but there are only a few where your chances are better than average.

The Red River in southern Manitoba may be your best bet in North America for catching a large walleye; the Red produces an awesome number of walleyes 10 pounds or heavier (101 Master Angler citations in a recent year, for example). These fish are migrants from Lake Winnipeg.

Generally dirty and roily, especially in spring and early summer, the Red River flows northward through farm country from the Dakotas through southern Manitoba into Lake Winnipeg. The hotbed of big-fish activity is in Manitoba, in the Selkirk area just north of the city of Winnipeg and below the Lockport Dam. However, big walleyes can be caught anywhere in the river, and succumb to a variety of presentations, with slow trolling one of the more reliable techniques for newcomers to this waterway.

October seems to be generally the best time to fish because

These anglers are about to land a citation-size walleye from the Red River. The Red may be the most prolific producer of walleyes over 8 pounds of any water in North America.

of the tremendous run of big walleyes migrating out of Lake Winnipeg. That runs starts in mid-September, when the water cools and the north winds begin to blow. The Winnipeg River, incidentally, which is about 60 miles away from Lockport, is another good producer of walleye. It does not seem to have as many large fish, but they are more aesthetically appealing, having an emerald-green coloration in the fall. Winnipeg River fish are locally called "greenbacks."

Actually, all walleyes here are called "pickerel," and fishing by local anglers is mostly done with so-called pickerel rigs, which sport a long-shanked bait hook for a nightcrawler and a small spinner blade. Drifting and stillfishing with live bait or jigs tipped with bait is also popular. Some plug trolling is done, mostly by visitors from the United States, and this merits attention as well.

The Red River is also known as one of the premier spots in North America for giant catfish. In Manitoba, the Red dominates the Master Angler citation list, and it rates as one of the best places to have a chance at catching a 20-pound or better specimen. The huge cats are almost exclusively taken on bait, predominantly chicken liver or gizzard shad chunks, fished along the bottom.

The best-known spot on the Red River is depicted here at the Selkirk Dam. This angler caught a large catfish at the base of the dam using a chunk of herring.

LAKE MEAD IS LOCATED
NEAR LAS VEGAS AND
SPANS BOTH ARIZONA
AND NEVADA.

*A rising sun greets a
summertime angler who
has already found that the
best schooling action of the
day on Lake Mead—as
well as the most
comfortable temperature—
can be had at dawn.*

LAKE MEAD
Nevada/Arizona

Two of the greatest wonders of North America exist near Lake Mead, one being Las Vegas, which needs no introduction to any adult on the continent, the other being the 726-foot-high Hoover Dam on the Colorado River—an engineering feat that still inspires awe fifty-five years after it was completed.

Many of the visitors to the gambling capital of the continent and to the engineering feat also find wonder in the waters that the dam contains, sampling its bounties time and again. Those bounties include striped bass, largemouth bass, catfish, crappie, and bluegills.

Bare and desolate country surrounds this lake in the desert, which stretches for roughly 105 miles, with 550 miles of shoreline snaking around canyons, coves, and various basins. The lake forks on the upper reaches, one shoot being the Overton Arm and the other being the Colorado River. All of this is part of the Lake Mead National Recreation Area, incidentally, in country where you are likely to be observed by bighorn sheep as you cast.

Like other impoundments on the Colorado River, Lake Mead and its 162,000 surface acres has many hideaways and offers diverse recreational opportunities, including a great deal of houseboat camping, cruising, and fishing.

Most of the angling attention here these days is focused on striped bass, which were initially introduced in 1968. Mead was noted for large stripers for a while, and although the occasional giant (over 30 pounds) is taken, the population now is composed of an enormous amount of small fish. Efforts are being made to restructure the population, but the quantity of fish nonetheless provides for some superb action at many times.

Mead is known for its striper schooling activities, especially those that take place early and late in the day in the warm months. This is considerate of these fish, as during a midsummer day it is routine for the temperature to soar past 100 degrees F here. On a good, typical summer morning, a party of striped bass anglers will have caught their fish by 9 o'clock and headed off the water.

Largemouth bass are doing better at Mead thanks to brush-planting efforts. The need for this pinpoints one of the deficiencies of this lake: steep shorelines, clear water, and very little cover. That makes the use of jigs and jigging spoons very popular, with the occasional chance to work a surface lure. The Las Vegas Wash, in the vicinity of the dam, is considered a good largemouth locale.

Below the dam, incidentally, the Colorado River carves its way through the Black Canyon for about 11 miles, headed toward Lake Mohave. This area is only accessible by boat (raft), and it provides an opportunity to catch big rainbow trout.

Houseboating is extremely popular on Lake Mead, allowing a means to get well out on the lake and camp in various locales, as well as for towing a fishing boat.

47

RIVERS INLET
British Columbia

Inaccessible by road, Rivers Inlet is situated to the east of Fitz Hugh Sound along the rugged coast of British Columbia. It is reached by twin-otter float plane or by private craft, which are usually trailered to Port Hardy on Vancouver Island and launched from there, with a two- to three-hour boat ride from that point. This remoteness, coupled with the fact that there are only a few lodges—situated on floats and firmly moored in the back of sundry bays and inlets—limits the number of fishermen who get to test the waters of Rivers Inlet and vie for the large salmon for which this locale is justly known.

Here, there are so many inlets, straits, and river mouths that an entire summer could be spent exploring—enjoying not only the fishing and the scenery but also the sight of bald eagles, humpback and killer whales, sea lions, and even the occasional grizzly bear. Put it all together, and you have one spectacular place to be angling through the summer.

The salmon fishery starts in mid-June at Rivers

SPANNING 40 MILES IN LENGTH AND 7 MILES ACROSS AT ITS ENTRANCE, **RIVERS INLET** IS SITUATED AT THE SOUTHEAST CORNER OF QUEEN CHARLOTTE SOUND, JUST NORTH OF CAPE CAUTION. IT IS PART OF THE INSIDE PASSAGE, A 1,600-KILOMETER (992-MILE) WATERWAY EXTENDING ALONG THE PACIFIC NORTHWEST FROM SEATTLE TO SKAGWAY.

The bay at the entrance to Rivers Inlet looks more like an inland mountain lake than the tidal saltwater setting that it actually is. At any time one is likely to see a whale breech.

A typical Rivers Inlet chinook draws wide smiles from this couple. Chinook, or king, salmon are the prime draw here, but coho, or spring, salmon are extremely popular as well.

There are no roads to Rivers Inlet, and access is achieved by water on a boat or by a float plane, which lands at the various floating lodges that are ensconced back in protected bays.

Inlet, when there is an early run of big king, or chinook, salmon. July is the month for best overall action, as small cohos show up as they follow baitfish schools. Cohos get larger as the season progresses, with the biggest, called "northern coho" being available in late August and September. These fish, pound for pound, are more exciting to catch than big chinooks, even though they don't grow as large. The big cohos are active, leaping, tenacious fighters, streaking rather than bulldogging, and some anglers prefer them to kings.

King salmon fishing is good from the beginning of the season through

the end of August, with the biggest fish usually being caught in late July and the first three weeks of August. Some of these fish are headed up the inlet to spawn in one of the four or five major tributaries (which itself makes for good angling opportunities) in the area, while others are migrating by as they head up or down the coast.

King salmon are the main attraction, not only because they are plentiful, but because they are large and strong. During the course of an average stay, it is a fair bet that one or more kings at or exceeding 40 pounds will be taken by someone in camp. Fish weighing 50 and 60 pounds are caught every year. Larger fish are possible. An 82.5-pound chinook caught at Rivers Inlet several decades ago stood as the all-tackle world record for a while. An 84-pounder was caught at Rivers Inlet in 1986. Two more 80-pounders were reportedly taken there in 1987.

No matter what size, these are impressive looking fish, deep-bodied and with thick girth, having fed well on herring, anchovies, and needlefish during their oceanic wanderings of several years. About thirty years ago, there were many canneries in Rivers Inlet and lots of traffic and commercial pressure. Virtually all of the canneries are now gone, although the specter of commercial driftnet fishing along the coast has recently been of considerable concern.

Salmon fishing at Rivers Inlet has actually been improving in general, in part due to a hatchery at the head of Rivers Inlet that was started in 1985. Already, 40-pound chinooks from hatchery stock have returned and been captured on rod and reel.

The silver, or coho, salmon, some weighing up to 25 pounds, come into the Inlet in two different runs, and the other species of Pacific salmon, chum, sockeye, and pink, are seasonally available as well. Pink and chum salmon show up from the middle to the end of July. The run builds in late July and peaks in early August.

One of the best locations for all salmon species at Rivers Inlet, especially for large chinook, is a spot known locally as "The Wall," west of Goose Bay along the southern shore. Here, the water drops sharply by a cliff to 90 feet, is 180 feet deep a short distance offshore, and then plummets to 400 feet 100 yards offshore. Fish congregate in this spot, allowing for specialized motor-mooching techniques using fresh-cut herring bodies for bait. Long rods, reels that hold a lot of fishing line, and heavy weights are used. The baits must be fished fairly deep, and a lot of attention is paid to achieving the proper roll of the herring, which is affected by current, tide, and boat movement. There is plenty of deep water in Rivers Inlet, and a lot of places worth fishing. The inlets of minor tributaries, back

Forty-five pounds of fish is a lot for any angler to heft, but it's no problem for this one, shown moments after landing the fish by "The Wall," a prominent Rivers Inlet salmon hole.

in secluded bays hemmed in by spruce and hemlock, are particularly appealing, and at times it's easy to forget you are fishing in salt water, not in a pristine mountain lake or deep in a fjord.

Early morning and late in the afternoon are preferred times for catching fish here, with some importance being attached to having lines in the water at low light. Many a large salmon is hooked before the sun pokes over the mountains and filters through the fog that wafts up the valleys. It is cold then, due to lack of sun and the fact that even in summer the water temperature is in the upper-40-degree F range. However, as with salmon everywhere, fish that have come into the inlet during the night are more agreeable before there is a lot of boat traffic and before the brighter light sends them deeper.

Fishermen in pursuit of king salmon journey to Rivers Inlet in July and August. There are many fishing sites to choose from here, including minor tributaries and hidden bays.

JUMPOFF POINTS FOR JOURNEYS INTO THE **BOUNDARY WATERS CANOE AREA** IN THE SUPERIOR NATIONAL FOREST OF NORTHERN MINNESOTA INCLUDE COOK, ELY, IŞABELLA, TOFTE, AND GRAND MARAIS.

A nice pike comes to net on one of the remote boundary lakes. A host of different species are found in the lakes in this area, although not all species are found in each lake.

BOUNDARY WATERS CANOE AREA
Minnesota

Not all great fishing locales are huge lakes or rivers, and not all such locations require big boats and a bulging tackle box. The Boundary Waters Canoe Area (BWCA) is tailor-made for anglers who aren't averse to a modest amount of wilderness trekking and gear toting and who'd like to savor campfires and evenings under the stars in the midst of the Minnesota-Ontario boundary area.

There are lakes galore in the BWCA, as you might expect in a region that is part of the Superior National Forest and which encompasses over 1 million acres stretching for some 150 miles. Most of the lakes are off-limits to motorized boats;

travel is accomplished by paddle power only. Portage trails through the woods provide access to lakes, but you have to carry your canoe as well as your fishing and personal equipment. Though the BWCA sees plenty of visitors, the number of fishermen has declined in recent years, probably because of the unwillingness of many anglers to make the effort that is required to travel and fish here.

More should make the effort. The quality of fishing is high. Good-size smallmouth bass, for example, are found in most of the lakes. There are a few largemouth bass, though catches are incidental. Pike and walleye inhabit most of the lakes as well, sometimes in great numbers, and lakers dwell in some of the deep waters.

The fish, however, won't jump into your boat, and you'll find that there are a lot of places that look good but are unproductive. Experienced anglers will do better, however guides are available in most regions of the BWCA, and this may be a good idea considering that a lot of time on a given trip will be consumed in simply getting from one place to the next, so you don't have as much time as you might think to scout out areas.

Fortunately, many of the fish are caught in fairly shallow waters. That's because the small, remote lakes aren't very deep and the water stays cool. Light tackle is the only way to go, primarily with spinning gear equipped with 4- to 8-pound line. Fly-casting tackle works well for shallow and surface fishing early in the season.

Good smallmouth bass fishing in a pristine and aesthetically attractive, remote environment is the allure for many anglers in the BWCA.

There is no doubt that you are in the wilderness on the BWCA waters. Canoe routes and trails for portaging crisscross throughout the entire area, where access is by canoe and foot only and no motors are permitted.

LAKE TEXOMA IS SITUATED ON THE OKLAHOMA-TEXAS BORDER, ABOUT 50 MILES NORTH OF DALLAS.

The striped bass population in Lake Texoma is exceptionally good, and the early and late hours are favored by many anglers.

LAKE TEXOMA
Oklahoma/Texas

According to some anglers, Lake Texoma is the premier striped bass lake in the United States. If you make that judgment based on sheer numbers of fish, particularly smaller ones, then few would disagree.

Actually, Lake Texoma has seen better times than the present, only because just a few years ago it had a nationally enviable reputation for large striped bass. Currently, it is not producing many leviathans—although large stripers are caught here every year—but the population of smaller fish is awesome. Severe floods in recent years have contributed to the explosion of small fish, as many of the large ones went over the dam. In fact, the best place to catch really big stripers now is in the tailrace waters below the Denison Dam. Large gizzard shad are used for bait there.

While natural bait is used in that locale, it used to be that trolling was the only way to catch stripers on Texoma, and that almost religiously involved the use of deep-diving plugs and trailing jigs. Today, trolling is not as popular as in the past, and casting with plugs is of foremost interest, particularly when the fish are schooling and there is opportunity to get stripers on top. That is a summer and fall proposition. Jigging, of course, is also very effective.

One of the odd twists in the striper boom on Lake Texoma is that it has taken the pressure off the black bass population, meaning that there are fewer people fishing for bass and that the angling for these species can be quite good.

Largemouth bass on this 91,200-acre impoundment are doing very well, and the smallmouth fishery has exploded. In fact, both the Texas and Oklahoma state records for smallmouth bass have been broken in the last few years by fish from this border lake.

With so much water spread over two states, plus the Red and Washita river arms, there are a lot of nooks and crannies to scour for bass. Those nooks also hold plenty of crappies and white bass, incidentally, plus catfish. Texoma has produced some gargantuan blue cats over the years and rates highly as a place for lunkers.

Largemouth bass have benefited from the angler concentration on stripers, as this Texoma fisherman can attest. Smallmouth bass are also present in Texoma.

shore locales. Muskies here are like muskies everywhere, not terribly abundant or cooperative, but a sometimes-catch, with special emphasis placed on fall angling when the water is cooler.

The better fishing spots include Buckhorn, Pigeon, and Stony Lakes for largemouth bass; Balsam and Buckhorn for smallmouths; Balsam, Pigeon, and Sturgeon for walleyes; and Pigeon and Stony for muskies. Rice and Scugog lakes are noted for all species.

This region is rich in history, incidentally, having been a major travel route for the likes of Samuel de Champlain and other explorers, as well as for the Iroquois and Huron tribes.

Transformed into a system of natural and manmade lakes linked by canals and locks, the area was once a vehicle for commerce but today is primarily a means of water control and source for recreational navigation.

Visitors will find the eastern end of the Kawarthas, including lakes Katchewanooka, Clear, Stony, and Lovesick to be the prettiest. The narrow and island-studded Hell's Gate junction of Clear and Stony lakes is particularly beautiful. And, with the possible exception of the main body of Sturgeon Lake, there are plenty of places to go if the wind kicks up. By studying navigation charts, one can find back bays, fingers, marshes, and offtrack hideaways to fish or explore.

Kawartha, incidentally, is an Indian word meaning "bright waters and happy lands," a perfect description of the area.

Cocktail time at Sturgeon Lake. There are few places in North America where boating is more vigorously pursued in all its forms than in the Kawarthas, which are a navigable part of the Trent-Severn Waterway and see passage by all types of craft.

LAKE OAHE
South Dakota

Some large bodies of water are known by reputation across the continent, and some, though having equal merit as angling shangri-las, just don't have the notoriety. The latter description befits Lake Oahe, which, although monstrous in size, generally gets a "Where's that?" comment from anglers everywhere outside of the upper Midwest. Well, it's in South Dakota, and you can't miss it on a map because it's 231 miles long with over 740,000 acres of water.

Swimming in that water are populations of gamefish that really are outstanding and which fit the interests of sportfishermen of all persuasions.

For the walleye buff, Oahe teems with marbleyes, including many in the 6- to 8-pound range and some in the 10-pound class. The big fish are prime in the fall, but spring fishing is also good, especially around tributaries. Good walleye angling also exists in the tailrace waters below the dam.

Lake Oahe is also a good spot for big northern pike. Several hundred over 15 pounds are caught annually, and 20- to 25-pounders are very possible. As with pike fishing in most locales, prime angling exists in the spring succeeding ice-out. Oahe also has a strong population of chinook salmon. Most of these fish are in midrange sizes, but some from 15 to 20 pounds are caught, with spring fishing holding most excitement.

LAKE OAHE IS PRIMARILY ACCESSED FROM PIERRE, THE CAPITAL OF SOUTH DAKOTA.

There are a number of different Lake Oahe species that will put a bend in a fishing rod. This angler is doing battle with a hefty walleye, of which this lake has plenty.

KEPIMITS LAKE IS ABOUT 100 MILES EAST OF WABUSH AND IS ACCESSED BY FLOAT PLANE FROM THERE OR ADJACENT LABRADOR CITY, SITE OF THE LARGEST IRON ORE MINE IN NORTH AMERICA.

The flowage between Lac Joseph and Kepimits Lake (in the background) is deep and swift, making it one of the prime places to fish. Thick stands of spruce line the lake, which is deep in the western bush country of Labrador.

KEPIMITS LAKE
Labrador

It is rather amazing to think that the western sector of Labrador, which encompasses 30,000 square miles and is absolutely loaded with lakes and rivers, has gone virtually unnoticed, despite having plenty of good, fairly shallow angling for a variety of species. Those include northern pike, lake trout, landlocked salmon, and brook trout, the latter a species with which this province is usually associated. In fact, most waters in this region have never been fished.

One, which only recently opened to anglers, is 16-mile-long Kepimits Lake, which can epitomize the type of experience that anglers most like to have: lots of action, including times when you have no idea what species of fish is likely to be caught next. At Kepimits, you might catch a salmon when you are after a laker, a pike when you are after a brook trout, a laker when you are after pike, and so forth. This is especially true in mid-June, when the season is just getting under way and most fish are located in shallow waters and near tributaries.

Kepimits adjoins Lac Joseph, a body of water that is 23 miles long and 18 miles wide at its largest points, and which has barely been scratched piscatorially. Both have many islands, countless bays, lots of deep water, plus the usual reefs and tributaries. Both are part of the enormous watershed of Smallwood Reservoir in the northern portion of western Labrador, and their water ultimately flows into that hydroelectric impoundment. The all-tackle world-record landlocked salmon (called "ouananiche"), a 22-pound, 11-ounce fish, was taken there.

Despite the hydro aspect, this is truly wilderness. Visitors have a good chance here of spotting black bear, moose, caribou, ospreys, bald eagles, martens, otters, and other wildlife among the thick but short fir and spruce, as well as observing the entrancing spectacle of the northern lights, or aurora borealis, in the sky on a summer night.

The area is accessed from mid-June through early September, with the most diverse fishing early in the season. Although a road was recently completed to Wabush, making vehicular traffic from Baie-Comeau, Quebec, possible for the first time, this is still virgin grounds and will remain so for a long time.

A lake trout, northern pike, and landlocked salmon (from the bottom), are on the cutting board at Kepimits, waiting to provide diners with an evening smorgasbord.

"Nature at its best" says the sign welcoming fishermen to the camp at Kepimits Lake, and indeed this is exactly the picturesque type of place that most anglers associate with Canada's northern wilds.

MUCH OF THE **COLUMBIA**'S GOOD FISHING IS IN THE LOWER REACHES, FROM THE MOUTH UP PAST THE BONNEVILLE DAM AND LAKE UMATILLA.

A walleye angler prepares his tackle at the launching site near Boardman, Oregon. The nearby waters of the Columbia produce some of the biggest walleyes anywhere in North America.

COLUMBIA RIVER
Oregon/Washington

From walleye to smallmouth bass to salmon and steelhead and sturgeon, the Columbia River is one fine place to go fishing.

Where walleyes are concerned, it has few peers in size and numbers elsewhere in North America. Walleyes up to 17 pounds have been produced in the Columbia, a lot of 10- and 12-pounders are caught annually, and a 23.5-pounder was reputedly taken in a net a few years back. But, as with walleyes everywhere, it has its slow moments, too.

The faster moments occur in the cooler weather of February, March, and April. Walleyes spawn in this period, and on the Columbia, the spawning activity is staggered. Late April through May is usually slack time, in part because of the postspawning doldrums but also because of an influx in cold water from snow-melt runoff. That, incidentally, affects the early smallmouth fishing, too, which is very good prior to the melt, but really slowed by the later cold water. The summer and fall periods are again good for both.

Walleyes are caught by trolling spinners nowadays, but jig fishing had been quite successful in the past. Smallmouth anglers find jigs to be the number-one items, with some reliance also on crankbaits and spinnerbaits. Lake Umatilla in the Boardman area is one of the focal points of activity. The smallmouth, incidentally, run to large sizes here, and state-record fish in the 8-pound category have been caught in the middle reaches of the river.

Traditionally, of course, the Columbia has been known for its salmon and steelhead. It gets all the Pacific salmon, with coho and chinook being the main items, and fishing in various parts of the main river and at the tributary flows.

The Columbia has been enjoying some of the best salmon runs in recent times in the past few years, and there is a possibility of hooking into fish in the 40-and 50-pound class. The spring run is essentially April and May; the fall run goes from September through November. The latter part of the fall is probably the best time to go for a trophy steelhead.

A lot of local anglers also pursue sturgeon in the Columbia, anchoring and drifting bait along the bottom. Three- to 6-footers are fairly common, and occasionally a much larger one, which has to be released, is hooked.

This is a big river that gets mighty rough, incidentally. When the wind whips up the river and fights the current, it gets serious. The Columbia River Gorge at Hood River is regarded as the sailboarding capital of North America, so you know it gets windy hereabouts.

A smallmouth bass angler works a rocky
shoreline on the Columbia River. Anglers
who get to know the various aspects of this
river enjoy extremely good smallmouth fishing.

LAKE OKEECHOBEE IS SMACK IN THE MIDDLE OF SOUTH-CENTRAL FLORIDA, NORTH OF THE EVERGLADES.

A hefty largemouth bass provides some excitement for an Okeechobee angler. Fish such as this one, weighing 10 pounds and more, are among the most coveted trophies in North America.

LAKE OKEECHOBEE
Florida

Of all the well-known largemouth bass waters in the state of Florida, none is more significant than Lake Okeechobee. Bass in the Big O, as it is often called, suffered when drought conditions in the early 1980s ago reduced the mean level of the lake to its lowest recorded level. This hurt the bass population by adversely affecting the spawn and shrinking habitat. Things turned around dramatically, then showed signs of reversing during low water in the late eighties, but have improved once again. Lake Okeechobee's bass fishing is still rated excellent.

This monstrous lake covers some 730 square miles of water. When the aforementioned drought ended and the lake returned to its normal level, a lot of new vegetation had been established along the shore. This meant new habitat and an increase in baitfish. When this happens, the bass spawns are excellent, and the net result is a lot of good largemouth bass action.

As you might expect, there are plenty of small bass in Okeechobee, but the fish grow up pretty fast. There are good numbers of 3- to 5-pound bass, and the ever-attractive lunkers— fish 8 to 10 pounds or better—are available. You can visit Lake Okeechobee knowing that you stand a very good chance of catching a trophy largemouth. Most people consider it to be the forerunner in both the state and the nation in producing big largemouth.

There really is no poor season to fish for bass on this lake. An overlooked season is summer, which is also the off-season for Florida's tourism trade. Good local anglers know that the summer produces reliable, stable bass angling; the weather may be a tad warm and sticky, but there are few cold fronts and unstable weather conditions to alter bass behavior (which is what happens to bass in all southern and shallow waters in the winter and early spring). The fish are much more predictable from midspring through midfall. This factor, plus the greater availability of accommodations and facilities in the summer, make it a good idea to keep off-season fishing in mind.

Because of its southern location, Okeechobee is often the least-affected Florida bass spot during late winter and early

spring, when a lot of snowbirds are in this state for vacation. It can offer fantastic fishing at that time, however, particularly when the weather is stable for a while. The fishing from September to December is also quite good.

Okeechobee's needlegrass and peppergrass flats concentrate largemouths during the spawning period (from February into April). The Big O is only 14 feet above sea level in normal conditions; it isn't very deep, yet bass move off the shallow flats after spawning and go into slightly deeper water. Personnel from local fisheries say that Okeechobee's bass populations move around from one season to another in the large lake. Because of this, it a good idea for the newcomer to hire a guide, especially for the first visit.

Lake Okeechobee's 200,000 surface acres of water make it a little difficult to pinpoint places to devote your bass-angling efforts. The Monkey Box area near Moonshine Bay is locally renowned, and the peppergrass flats between Observation Shoals and Clewiston as well as the channels and cuts from Clewiston to Okeetantee, are among the more popular fishing locales.

Live golden shiners account for a majority of the giant bass taken at the Big O, especially in the winter, when the temper-

The ever-abundant hayfields of Lake Okeechobee provide fertile grounds for largemouth bass and are worked thoroughly by thousands of anglers every season.

Though unable to venture very far from the rim canal that rings Okeechobee because of the morning fog, this angler still managed to land one of the prime specimens of largemouth bass for which this lake is renowned.

The shallow nature of Lake Okeechobee lends itself to wade-fishing. In distant locales, wading anglers are transported by air-boat and dropped off, then picked up a bit later and delivered to a new site.

Lake Okeechobee, ctd.

ature drops and the fish become somewhat reluctant feeders. But when things have stabilized, surface lures provide exciting fishing, and the shallow cover can provide decent fly-fishing. Plastic worms remain the top artificial by a wide margin, but floating minnow plugs, crankbaits, weedless spoons, and spinnerbaits at times are productive. Schools of fish occasionally chase shad, and the bass can be readily caught on a crankbait or other plug or surface lure. Heavy tackle is a good idea; you always have a chance of busting a big bass in the cover, and you will have to muscle it out.

Okeechobee also has good fishing for bluegills, crappies, and catfish, for those who are interested in the smaller species and something tasty for the pan. Bluegill (called "bream" here) fishing is prime in the spring, and often the shorelines of the lake's lengthy canals are lined with spawning beds. There are plenty of catfish, and these creatures are fished commercially as well here. And black crappies (known as "speckled perch" here) are taken throughout the year, but especially during winter.

BIG SAND LAKE IS
ACCESSED FROM
WINNIPEG VIA THOMPSON
BY WHEELED PLANE AT A
PRIVATE AIRSTRIP. IT IS A
SHORT DISTANCE BY AIR
FROM SOUTH INDIAN LAKE.

BIG SAND LAKE
Manitoba

It occurred to me that
there was something very
special about Big Sand Lake
in northern Manitoba when,
one morning a few years
ago, I took a walk on an
island about 12 miles from
camp. I covered about three-
quarters of a mile of sandy

preceding page:
Big Sand has walleyes that must be stacked on top of each other like cordwood, according to the author's experiences. The catch displayed by this guide is a typical one for the lake.

A fine northern pike comes to boat at Big Sand Lake. Virtually unfished for many years, the lake has recently been opened to sport angling.

beach, and at one point stood still to watch a bald eagle fly overhead, answering the cries of its young, while in the sand nearby were fresh moose tracks; 50 yards offshore was a group of twelve loons, diving for food and calling raucously to one another; and down the beach a sandpiper hunted for small prey. One could almost forget about fishing.

Well, almost. Later that day, two of us took a five-minute boat ride from the deluxe Big Sand Lake lodge to the outlet of Katimew Lake, one of many tributaries to Big Sand, and caught more walleyes than I imagined could be possible in 100 yards of water. Moreover, we caught them in good sizes and on every conceivable type of lure. A walleye angler's paradise for sure.

The walleyes in this lake—and the ones we caught—average in the 3- and 4-pound class and are readily caught on crankbaits and jigs. There are bigger fish, however, and there will be walleyes of trophy sizes soon, as the lodge here is practicing a strict no-kill (except for small fish for shore lunch) barbless-hook-only angling policy. Once commercially fished by the Indians, Big Sand Lake has been off limits for some time, and only sport angling is now practiced, and even that is just getting started.

Additionally, Big Sand has *beaucoup* northern pike, and this holds great merit, too. I caught pike to 17 pounds during my midsummer visit a few years ago, but was assured by native guides that several dozen at or over 20 pounds were caught in the spring. Cabbageweeds abound in bays and along points and deep shorelines, making for great habitat for these sulking predators.

Big Sand is a large lake, nearly 50 miles long, and has plenty of places that have not been fished much at all, not to mention the good-size grayling (3-pounders) that exist on the South Seal River, which is a pleasant, two-hour boat ride from the lodge. Lake trout and whitefish round out the possibilities, though little is known about either here.

MONTAUK POINT
New York

MONTAUK POINT IS AT THE EASTERNMOST TIP OF NEW YORK'S DENSELY POPULATED LONG ISLAND.

Bluefish provide the main attraction for the bulk of anglers at Montauk and vicinity these days. This angler, shown on a Montauk dock, is carting off fish that he and several others took in a morning's outing.

Montauk Point has such good fishing for a variety of species that it has to rate as the premier gamefishing port on the entire East Coast. Montauk and its environs are like a magnet for migrating gamefish, which find the many rips, reefs, and banks in the area conducive to foraging. The availability of some species is as dependent on currents and water temperatures as much as on fish stocks and bait, but area anglers are easily able to head offshore to the deep-water canyons or to north or south attractions, as well as find productive fishing inshore and in close proximity to the Point. The waters here are especially noted for some giant catches.

Few get more gigantic than the 3,427-pound great white shark landed here in the mid-1980s. Until surpassed in spring of 1990 by an Australian great white, this was the biggest fish ever caught on rod and reel.

Since the mid-1970s, Montauk has been a hotbed for pursuing various toothy creatures, with blue sharks being most abundant, followed by brown sharks and hammerheads. Makos are most popular, however, both for great sport and good table fare. The current all-tackle world-record mako, a 1,080-pounder, was caught off Montauk in 1979.

Both bluefin and yellowfin tuna are caught here. The bluefins don't rival the Maritime Provinces of Canada in size, but there are giants caught each year—most in the fall and likely to be in the 500-pound class—as well as a lot of subgiant-size fish. Tuna fishing at Montauk used to be a trolling proposition, but chunking—chumming at anchor with chunked, rather than ground-up, fish— is the mainstay now, with butterfish, bunker, and herring the preferred baits. This takes place in the distant canyon grounds, the Butterfish Hole, and the Texas Tower.

Yellowfins are mostly caught in the summer. In some years there is an abundance of 50- to 70-pound fish; in others, fish

In the fall, when the tuna are in, these mighty fish put a lot of strain on a fishing rod. This angler is battling a giant bluefin that took a chunk of fish bait amid a fleet of boats anchored in Montauk waters.

in the 100- to 120-pound class are possibilities. They are mainly caught on the top of banks where bait is abundant, some being 10 to 12 miles from the Point. Exceptional yellowfin angling through the fall is frequently had well offshore. Other offshore fish include big-eye tuna, albacore, bonito, dolphin, swordfish, and marlin.

Inshore fishing opportunities are very good from surf fishing to reef trolling. Striped bass have been a mainstay here, with many big fish, including the former 76-pound all-tackle world record, having been taken locally, but that fishery is not back to former levels.

However, bluefish are abundant at Montauk and in the entire metropolitan New York-New Jersey area from generally the middle of May through November. The area from the Point to Rhode Island's Block Island is especially notable, and there are many rips and ledges that regularly produce. Jigging and trolling are popular techniques, and cut bait is also widely used. Some casting is done as well, when bluefish are working a school on the surface or when they roam the shallows and become the target of surf pluggers.

LAC BEAUCHENE
Quebec

Two anglers fish out of the author's boat on Lac Beauchene. This 12-mile-long lake has some exceptional angling opportunities for several species of fish.

Big smallmouth bass and near-virgin waters are an appealing combination to anglers who fancy the fish that is not one of North America's largest-growing finny creatures, but undoubtedly one of its gamest. Surely one of the best places on the continent to fulfill both aspirations is a little-known reserve in the southwestern corner of Quebec. Here, a fish is not worthwhile to local anglers unless it is a brook trout. There is plenty of opportunity for some extraordinary angling for that species, but for visiting anglers that is merely

LOCATED IN THE KIPAWA REGION OF SOUTHWESTERN QUEBEC, **BEAUCHENE** IS A FIVE-AND-A-HALF HOUR-DRIVE NORTH OF TORONTO, NINETY MINUTES FROM MATTAWA, AND SEVENTY-FIVE MINUTES FROM NORTH BAY.

a bonus, the main draw being the plentitude and high average size of *Micropterus dolomieui*.

Perhaps the most notable thing about La Reserve Beauchene is the place itself, for it signifies what many anglers today want and what some astute lodge owners and outfitters are striving to supply: good fishing in an aesthetically pleasing setting and attention to improving and preserving the resource so it will last.

At the heart of the matter is 12-mile-long Lac Beauchene. It is the largest of numerous lakes in La Reserve Beauchene, which is 45,000 acres of land where the hunting and fishing rights are privately and exclusively leased from the provincial government by an outfitter. Recreation, which can be enjoyed by the public for a fee, is strictly managed. For many years, the land was leased to an American distillery and used only by its guests. It then went to a Quebec family, which instituted and refined some of the present catch-and-release regulations; a few years ago, the family sold the lease to Ontario angler Dick Waterous.

Bass are the main attraction from early June on, which is a bit ironic. These fish aren't native to the reserve waters, and were reputedly stocked by the original leaseholder some sixty years ago. Their presence is not only due to the excellent habitat, but also to the fact that they were unmolested by local fishermen.

So the bass evolved into a hardy population of chunky fish. While they can be a bit elusive or hard to entice here, they can also be very easy, and they do some things that you don't see very often. At times, for example, the big bass school. They also are found in a high average size, especially early in the season, when they are shallower and more vulnerable. When I was there recently, friends and I caught

Small lakes and ponds in the area offer wilderness fishing experiences and an opportunity to have good success.

smallmouths over 4 pounds every day (three in one afternoon), and on Petit Lac Beauchene, our bass averaged 3 pounds, which are impressive credentials. Jigs and minnow-imitating plugs are top bass lures here, with standard spinning tackle being in the light class, with 4- to 8-pound line.

Smallmouth bass are not all that the reserve waters offer, however. Even the most unlucky fisherman could catch lake trout at Lac Beauchene if he trolled a spoon or minnow plug along the shorelines long enough. There are many in the 3- to 5-pound range here, and in May these fish are very shallow and relatively easily caught. Five other lakes on the reserve also possess lakers.

Although we primarily caught walleyes by accident while jigging for bass, we did find a spot or two that reliably produced walleyes. Those fish averaged between 3 and 4 pounds, but fish up to 10 pounds have been taken in Lac Beauchene, while 10- to 12-pounders have come from one of the reserve's other lakes.

Northern pike are an incidental catch for the most part and are generally small, although fish up to 17 pounds have been caught here. Not small at all are the brook trout that inhabit several of the lakes on the reserve property. These are relatively small lakes, set aside for brook trout management, and there are fish to 8 pounds in them. Smaller fish are there, too, but for some reason the lakes don't yield a lot of brook trout (known as "speckled trout" here), but a high average size. The chance of catching a 4-

Some exceptionally good brook trout are caught in the reserve lakes each season. Roger Tucker proudly displays a 4-pound fish.

pounder or better is good.

Owner Dick Waterous was drawn to the area primarily for its brook trout, but has recognized the value of all the fisheries and is working to enhance and preserve them. He has formulated specific catch-and-release guidelines, fishing rules, and management objectives. Anglers are allowed to keep only one trophy fish of a protected species, adhering to minimum sizes.

Also noteworthy is the abundant wildlife on the reserve lands and waters, from plenty of mournful-sounding loons to moose, otters, and eagles. Considering that you can drive here and bring your own boat, it all adds up to one of the finest sporting experiences on the continent.

A huge smallmouth, such as this 5-pounder held by Lac Beauchene veteran Dick Bengraff, is the main attraction through the summer months.

THE TOWNS OF CLINTON, SHIRLEY, AND GREER'S FERRY RING **GREER'S FERRY LAKE**, WHICH IS ACCESSED FROM U.S. HIGHWAY 25 AND STATE HIGHWAY 92.

This is the kind of fish that makes springtime headlines for Greer's Ferry. The possibility of catching such a big walleye is especially strong in late winter, when the fish are making a spawning run up the creeks.

GREER'S FERRY LAKE
Arkansas

One of the prettiest places to fish in mid-America is a moderate-size impoundment nestled in the eastern foothills of the Ozark Mountains. There, Greer's Ferry Lake offers year-round sport for a host of gamefish, though it has been most renowned for its large walleyes.

The walleyes get attention because they come in large bundles. Not a lot of walleyes, mind you, but big ones. The late-winter spawning run of walleyes sends fish from 17 to 22 pounds up the tributaries sporadically, and occasionally someone up a creek catches a fish to write home about. A few small and intermediate sizes are caught, yet many people have been waiting for the next world-record walleye (over 25 pounds) to come from here.

Greer's Ferry is a Corps of Engineers impoundment that ranges between 31,000 (low pool) and 40,000 (flood-control pool) acres of surface water. It was completed in December 1962, and its tributaries are the various forks of the Little Red River, which is part of the White River drainage.

Water temperature is the all-important factor in the tributaries. After some stable warm weather and a heavy rainfall, which may occur from early to late March, the rivers and their immediate downstream areas have a significantly higher temperature than the lake. From the low-50-degree-F range on, things begin to happen. Black bass become active, and white bass and hybrid stripers migrate in schools into the tributaries prior to spawning.

Late spring and summer fishing is best for black bass, and fall is notable for white bass and hybrid stripers. The upper and lower ends of this lake are connected by a narrows, and the south end of the lake, between markers 2 and 7, seems to offer the best hybrid and white bass fishing from September until mid-November. Schools of these fish roam widely

Greer's Ferry is noted for its bass fishing and also for its hybrid striper population. This striper was caught in the winter in a timbered Greer's Ferry creek.

after bait. Though a concentration of fish at times may be found in deep water and caught by vertical spoon jigging, most of the angling then consists of trolling or casting to surfacing schools of fish.

Greer's Ferry is the number-one hybrid striper fishery in Arkansas, and one of the tops in the United States for this particularly robust, fighting fish. Catching 8-pounders has been common in the past, and larger sizes are possible. Perhaps the very best hybrid fishing is had at a time of year that often draws few visitors: from mid-March through December. Jump-fishing and shallow trolling are the rule then, and the biggest fish of the year are usually taken.

ATLIN IS ALMOST ON THE BORDER OF BRITISH COLUMBIA AND THE YUKON TERRITORY, AND IS REACHED VIA WHITEHORSE.

At Atlin Lake, a fisherman admires the grayling that he caught on a dry fly. Grayling, lake trout, and pike are plentiful there.

The high mountain rivers offer outstanding scenery and plenty of solitude. The only companion for the day, in fact, could be a grizzly bear—which wise fishermen carefully avoid.

ATLIN
British Columbia

Getting to your fishing grounds by helicopter is an exhilarating experience, but a rather common one inland in northern British Columbia, where the rivers are remote and wild, the salmon large and strong. Here, the only way to access the wild-river hideaways is to, well, drop in on them.

So you cram into the chopper at Atlin, fishing rod tube strapped securely to the struts, and inside of a minute you are buzzing over mountaintops and through valleys flanked by snowy, craggy peaks. You pass over gorges and rapids deeper into the wilderness, and suddenly, in the distance, nestled amid the poplars, you can see the few faded-yellow specks of the tent camp that will be your home for a few days, on a sand and gravel bar that you will share with only your companions, bald eagles, and possibly a grizzly bear, which you will give wide berth.

Here, the steelhead run thick in late April and May, then the salmon follow, with Dolly Varden and rainbow trout providing occasional surprises. King, or chinook, salmon are the most coveted fish, but there are several species of salmon that will be in the river, depending on the time of the year—all of which have made a lengthy and rather remarkable journey to fulfill their procreational destiny and are met by a few fishermen, wading the swift flows and fishing with fly, heavy spoon, or bottom-bouncing plug beneath a snow-capped mountain vista.

Those mountains form a divide that separates Pacific and Arctic watersheds, incidentally, the result being that rivers on one side flow northerly, and on the other side southwesterly through Alaska.

Meanwhile, inland, perhaps 40 miles from Atlin and accessed only by float plane, is one of the finest lakes in western Canada. This is Hall Lake, a narrow, 12-mile-long body of water that features a lot of rocky shoals and a fair number of islands. It has barely been fished, but compares extremely favorably with its better-known neighbors, Atlin, Teslin, and Gladys lakes.

From early June until early September, the attraction here is lake trout, including 15- to 20-pounders; pike up to 20 pounds; and more grayling than you ever thought existed. Couple a visit here with a wild-river salmon experience, and you simply have the best that the Pacific Northwest has to offer.

This angler is bringing a chinook salmon into the gravel bar to unhook and release. Chinooks are the main quarry, but coho salmon and steelhead are also seasonally very popular.

Mountain peaks topped with snow provide a picture-postcard image behind the placid waters of Hall Lake. It is a sight that fishermen enjoy throughout the summer.

THE **ST. LAWRENCE RIVER**
BORDERS ONTARIO AND
NEW YORK, WITH THE
MOST PROMINENT
LOCALES FOR FISHING
BEING AT CAPE VINCENT,
CLAYTON, AND
ALEXANDRIA BAY IN NEW
YORK, AND KINGSTON
AND GANANOQUE IN
ONTARIO.

*Bass fishing and the St.
Lawrence River are nearly
synonymous in anglers'
minds, because the fish
are so abundant here.
This image was taken
near Chippewa Bay.*

ST. LAWRENCE RIVER
New York

The St. Lawrence River is one of the great North American fishing locales that is no secret. Steeped in history, tradition, and fishing renown, this is one of the places that has been in the sportfishing limelight since ever there was a limelight. Its natural resources were of tremendous value as long ago as 1535, when French explorer Jacques Cartier discovered it while looking for the Northwest Passage to the Orient.

But it is the 52-mile-long section of the St. Lawrence called the Thousand Islands—known to the Mohawk Indians as the "garden of the great spirit"—which has produced not only the famous salad dressing of that name, but some of the continent's foremost bass and muskellunge fishing.

If you are not familiar with the St. Lawrence River, you might be inclined to think of it as a typical river, featuring pools, eddies, and riffles. Think again. It is more like a mammoth lake, holding half a million surface acres of water. Also known as the St. Lawrence Seaway, the river flows northeasterly from Lake Ontario for 700 miles and is used as a shipping channel for colossal freighters carrying assorted cargoes from Great Lakes ports. It is 200 feet deep in spots, several miles wide at most points, and there are over 1,600 islands in the Thousand Islands sector, the largest of which is 21 miles long.

The prime angling interests in this great body of water are smallmouth bass, largemouth bass, walleyes, northern pike, and muskellunge. The St. Lawrence is a fabled muskie water and has been renowned for its large specimens. The all-tackle world-record muskie, 69 pounds, 15 ounces, was caught somewhere in the Thousand Islands stretch in 1957, and several 60-pounders were caught here during the heyday of the 1950s. No other single locale has been as closely identified with mighty muskellunge as the St. Lawrence.

The huge fish have not been caught here in recent years, however, and angling interest has shifted to more abundant species, especially to large salmon in nearby Lake Ontario. Still, 30- to 40-pound muskies are landed every year by the dedicated trollers, with much emphasis still placed on tradi-

Successful muskie fishermen prepare to revive a fish that was caught at Gananoque Narrows one fall day.

tional locales, such as Hinckley Shoal off Carleton Island and Forty Acre Shoals off Gananoque. This is almost exclusively a trolling fishery, partaken of from September through early November.

Many more people ply the St. Lawrence for bass. Area chambers of commerce have long billed the local waters as the "smallmouth bass capital of the world," and while some would dispute this claim, there is no arguing the fact that the river has a tremendous population of smallmouths, thanks in part to a phenomenal quantity of rocky bars, shoals, bluffs, and island heads near deep water with plenty of current.

Largemouths, too, are abundant, in the main river along deep grass beds and weed lines as well as back in the weedy and lily-pad-filled bays and creeks. Lake of the Isles at Wellesley Island is one of the most noted largemouth areas.

Jigs and live bait are the foremost presentations here for bass, but the entire gamut of bass tactics and tackle are applicable. Good fishing can be had almost all season long from mid-June until November.

Northern pike, though not particularly large here, are abundant and provide a good spring and winter quarry. Walleyes were once abundant, then nonexistent, and appear to be on the verge of reestablishing a major population. In a few more years, this river could be a hot walleye producer and source of large fish as well.

Large for most anglers, this St. Lawrence River muskellunge is less than half of the size of the world-record fish, which was caught in these waters several decades ago.

CHANTREY INLET IS IN THE KEEWATIN DISTRICT OF THE NORTHWEST TERRITORIES, ABOUT 1,500 MILES FROM FORT FRANCIS, ONTARIO.

A pile of rocks, used by Inuits to identify good fishing locales, stands guard over the Back River where it empties into Chantrey Inlet in the background.

CHANTREY INLET
Northwest Territories

It is only fished a few weeks out of the year, but Chantrey Inlet holds great memories of large lake trout and arctic char for its visitors.

Located in the Arctic tundra on the mainland Northwest Territories, Chantrey Inlet is the place where the mighty Back River courses through Franklin Lake. It attracts a prodigious run of big char (10 to 20 pounds) in early July as the ice leaves, and hosts scores of lake trout—including specimens that have topped the 60-pound mark—the rest of the season until mid-August. Most of the trout are in the 10- to 20-pound range, but there's a good chance here of getting one from 30 to 40 pounds. Grayling, too, exist along the shoreline in less tumultuous water and in two nearby small lakes.

Swift water and back eddies provide challenging moments for shore or boat anglers hooked to char or lakers, with most anglers using heavy spoons to troll or jigs for casting and drifting. This is not the place to try light tackle, fly-fishing, or gear of questionable endurance. Deep, rapid water, a boulder-strewn bottom, and extremely hard-fighting fish combine to provide some of the most demanding freshwater fishing and boating.

FLORIDA KEYS
Florida

Key Largo, Islamorada, Marathon, and Key West are legendary saltwater fishing locales, as are "the Keys" in general. This is where the big three of the flats—bonefish, permit, and tarpon— are the venerated quarry.

The Florida Keys stretch south and west bordering Florida Bay toward the mainland and tucking into the Gulf of Mexico. North of Key West, shallow flats extend well into the Gulf; to the south, the Gulf Stream is just a short distance away, sweeping by the Keys into the Florida Straits. Reefs, wrecks, and extensive shallow water areas offer diverse fishing opportunities in all seasons, while the blue water beckons those in search of billfish. Some boaters venture out to the Marquesas Islands or to the Dry Tortugas as well.

The upper Keys and Florida Bay have greater concentrations of bonefish and somewhat larger fish, particularly from Islamorada to Marathon. Bonefish in the 6-pound range are common, and larger fish are possible, as attested to by the eight line-class world records that have been established

Bonefish are pursued along the shallow flats of the Keys all year long. Fly-rodding for them is standard, with some anglers wading and some fishing from skiffs.

here. The gray ghost of the flats is caught all-year long on the ocean shallows of the Keys and in Florida Bay. However, cold fronts cause their temporary disappearance in the winter and early spring. Angling for bonefish is good from April through December, with larger bonefish from late summer through fall.

Many record-size permit have been caught in these waters, especially in the vicinity of Key West. Permit are less prominent in Florida Bay, but more numerous at the far end of the Keys. Spring and early summer are good times for seeking these fish on the flats, although they are also caught in deeper waters around reefs and ship-

reaches seventy-five degrees F. May and June are excellent, while April can be good if the weather has been favorable.

Sailfish are quite plentiful in the upper Keys early in the year; they're found in the lower Keys from November through winter. Blue marlin are sought in the lower Keys in fall, with sizes ranging up to 400 pounds. The summer is good for large dolphins offshore. And various types of tuna are part of the sportfishing take.

The spring is prime tarpon time in the Keys, and fish like this are a favorite quarry of anglers.

wrecks. Wrecks are, in fact, abundant, and the fishing there for various species is quite popular with many fishermen who bring their own boats.

Tarpon, of course, are a main quarry for visitors. They are found in many locales throughout the Keys, including the backwaters of Florida Bay and over toward Flamingo, as well as in the Marquesas Islands out in the Gulf. Key West has a heralded run of big tarpon in the winter, and a lot of records have been set there.

Tarpon in the Keys generally run under 100 pounds, yet there are plenty of them, plus the bigger ones over 100. They usually show up about the time that the water temperature

Dolphin may be the most acrobatic of all saltwater fish, and this one is doing its best to uphold that image. Light-tackle angling for these and other fish is especially prevalent in the Keys.

THE UPPER **DELAWARE RIVER** BORDERS NEW YORK AND PENNSYLVANIA FOR 75 MILES FROM PORT JERVIS TO HANCOCK.

A shad comes to net on the Delaware near Port Jervis. Shad are abundant from late April through June and attract a lot of angling attention.

DELAWARE RIVER
New York/Pennsylvania

Select an answer from the following choices: The Delaware River is a) one of the finest wild trout rivers in the northeastern United States; b) the best place for American shad on the East Coast; c) a terrific smallmouth bass river; or d) all of these.

It is all of these, according to some, and while there may be debate as to the degree of superlatives attached to this, there is no question that this river, especially the upper reaches which split the New York and Pennsylvania boundary in the Catskill Mountains and its foothills, is a top angling draw.

Actually, the entire main stem of the river, from Hancock, New York, down to Delaware Bay, has much to recommend it, but the upper reach, which was designated as a National Wild and Scenic River in 1978, is most notable aesthetically and piscatorially, as are the upriver tributaries, which include the east and west Branches of the Delaware, and the Lackawaxen, Mongaup, and Neversink rivers.

Perhaps no species is more abundant in the Delaware nor more energetically pursued than American shad, albeit for a short period of time. Shad migrate all the way upriver and into the upper tributaries to spawn, with the bulk of the fishing activity taking place from late April through mid-June. These fish are frequently caught in 4- to 6-pound sizes, occasionally in great numbers, and they are pursued by both boat and wading fishermen, with most attention paid around Port Jervis, Sparrowbush, Barryville, Lackawaxen, and Narrowsburg.

Although trout are found throughout, the section from Hancock to Callicoon is the prime trout water, with a good population of brown trout and rainbow trout, plus the occa-

sional brookie. These are predominantly wild fish, and there is a good chance of getting some in the 16- to 20-inch range, which is considered exceptional anywhere in the Northeast. Rainbows are more common, and fly-fishing is the preferred method, although other artificials and bait are used.

Smallmouths are found throughout this river, but good fishing exists in the upper river, and especially south of Callicoon, where the water temperatures are especially favorable. Walleyes inhabit the river, too, although they are not intensely pursued; some large walleyes are taken, with most angling occurring in spring and fall.

The access situation is not a particularly good one on the Delaware. It is limited, and one cannot cross private property without permission. Several public-access spots are located on each side of the upper river. Fishing during the day in the summer, especially weekends, is hampered by tremendous canoe and raft traffic; this is a very popular floating waterway.

Duncan Barnes, Editor of Field & Stream magazine, plays a fish on the upper Delaware River near Hankins. This cold-water section of the river provides prime trout fishing.

LAKE POWELL IS LOCATED IN NORTHERN ARIZONA AND SOUTHERN UTAH. IT IS ACCESSED FROM FIVE LOCALES, THE MOST FREQUENT BEING PAGE, ARIZONA.

The steepness of the countryside extends to the water as well, and much fishing effort is directed along the shorelines.

LAKE POWELL
Utah/Arizona

There's little doubt that 186-mile-long Lake Powell deserves its reputation as the "bass capital of the West." Yet it also has other notable fish species. And, in terms of angling enjoyment, scenery, and pure grandeur, Powell is simply awesome. If you are a shore-oriented angler, as most people are, you may be happy to know that this Utah impoundment has more shoreline than Lake Michigan, which is the sixth-largest lake in the world. Then again, you may not relish the knowledge that Lake Powell has 1,900 miles of shoreline, because that means a too-many-choices potpourri of great-looking places to fish.

Even if you diligently fish Lake Powell, you'll likely be sidetracked by some of the greatest scenery in the United States. Natural geological wonders, Indian ruins, petroglyphs, hundred-foot cliffs, towering mountains, and other eye-opening splendors are ample cause for distraction. The most famous natural attraction is Rainbow Bridge National Monument, which, at 290 feet high, is the world's tallest stone arch.

Lake Powell was created in 1963 when the Glen Canyon Dam across the Colorado River was completed. The lake extends from Page, Arizona, into Utah and is fed by three major rivers: the Colorado, San Juan, and Escalante. It is also edged by many canyons, which are larger than the lakes that most visiting anglers ordinarily fish in their locales. There are ninety-six named, navigable tributary canyons; eight major bays; and dozens of smaller, nameless waterways.

Lake Powell is a place where one can get lost, accidentally or on purpose, and find a hideaway that offers excellent relaxation, contemplation, and fishing values. Many visitors to this lake rent houseboats to tour and fish the lake for a week or more at a time, often bringing a fishing boat in tow. Although there are trout, walleyes, crappies, pike, catfish, smallmouth bass, bluegills, and other fish species in Powell, the largemouth bass and striped bass are the most popularly pursued.

Anglers have to be versatile and adaptable to fish successfully here, especially if their quarry is largemouth bass. The water is very clear, sometimes to 20 feet deep, in the main areas, necessitating the use of fairly light line, yet it can be dirty with submerged trees in some of the coves, requiring heavier tackle. In the spring, you can go to the upper end of the lake and there will be ice-cold water feeding in from the snow-melt runoff, while at the opposite end of the lake, the water will be warm enough for the bass to be spawning.

Visiting anglers need sportfishing sonar on their boat to properly probe the Lake Powell shores. Many bluffs and sheer rock walls look inviting, but you can seldom tell what's below from a look at the shore. The underwater ledges, dropoffs, and craggy cliffs often hold bass, and it's necessary to fish very close to cover. That may explain why jigs and plastic worms are especially favored throughout the season.

Although there is hardly any vegetation to be found in the lake, submerged trees are found in many spots, particularly in coves, and the treetops may come close to the surface.

Lake Powell is one of the most geologically magnificent places in North America to fish. Narrow canyons, as seen to right of center here, extend far back off the main lake in many places, offering shelter, fishing opportunity, and pleasant mooring for overnight houseboat travelers.

A fisherman tries his luck in a serene Lake Powell canyon. Many people explore Lake Powell by houseboat, towing or bringing some type of fishing vessel with them to work the distant waters.

Largemouth bass, as this angler is unhooking, are the foremost gamefish in Lake Powell, and are intensively sought by anglers. Striped bass are another major quarry.

Flooded or submerged brush offer inviting flipping targets, and flipping is a productive technique for largemouth bass along some rocky shores as well. At times, spinnerbaits, crankbaits, and surface plugs contribute to success, but the ultraclear water of this impoundment mandates delicate presentations much of the time. Bait fishermen here are keen on using live waterdogs, which are salamanders.

Many anglers seek out more turbid water in the creeks and rivers, especially in the vast reaches of the San Juan River. This region seems to yield some of the heaviest bass in Lake Powell, but that may have to do more with the amount of angling attention than other factors.

The early part of the season is considered the most productive bass fishing time. March, April, and May offer good action in fairly shallow water. Later in the season a lot of angling will be from 15 to 40 feet deep for largemouths.

Lake Powell was the last of the Colorado River impoundments to get a striper fishery going, and biologists at the fisheries expect that real heavyweights (40-plus-pounders) may become more common in time. There are presently many small stripers, as well as those from 5 to 15 pounds, to be caught, as well as the odd 20-pounder. The Colorado River below the dam, incidentally, down to Lees Ferry, offers some excellent fishing opportunities for rainbow, cutthroat, and brook trout, in water that is continuously in the chilly, mid-40-degrees-F range.

THE **FRENCH RIVER** IS
SITUATED IN SOUTHERN
ONTARIO, NORTH OF
TORONTO AND SOUTH OF
SUDBURY, AND IT FLOWS
INTO THE GEORGIAN BAY
AREA OF LAKE HURON.

*A French River guide
proudly hoists a small
muskie prior to releasing it.
This drainage for Georgian
Bay produces some muskies
far larger than this one.*

FRENCH RIVER
Ontario

Flowing out of Lake Nipissing and into Georgian Bay and traversing a distance of some 110 kilometers (about 68 miles), the French River is rich in many ways. Historically, it conveyed French missionaries and explorers and later, pioneers and tradesmen; geologically, it exhibits preglacial land of the Canadian Shield formations; recreationally, it supplies countless hours of high-quality boating and fishing in one of the most beautiful areas of southern Canada.

The French is a different river in its upper and lower sections, and its reaches include a series of falls and rapids; some narrow, granite-walled sections; bays that have modest flowage and look more like lakes; and a delta

with a course of channels leading to the big water. The fishing experiences are also diverse, as it happens, and include the species that southern Canada, and the province of Ontario in particular, are so widely noted for smallmouth bass, walleyes, northern pike, and muskellunge. Each of these is remarkable in its own right.

Walleyes, called "pickerel" here, are the most popularly sought fish of the French and its tributaries. These fish evidently migrate to and from Georgian Bay, with late May, June, July, and August being particularly good for angling below the rapids of the lower river out in the delta area, and July night fishing being best for big walleye. The fall months are best for walleye in the river proper. These fish have the potential to grow to 10-pound proportions, and there are a number of monsters taken each season. Smallmouths are taken throughout the same period, with fish over 4 pounds

possible; July is a time to find lots of fish as well.

Muskies are the river's most fickle fish, but they, too, exist in impressive sizes. A 59-pound, 7-ounce fish was caught in 1989 by Art Barefoot in the Hartley Bay area, making it the largest fish ever from this waterway on rod and reel. Quite a few muskies in the 30- and near 40-pound class have come from here in the last decade, yet surprisingly it is not fished very hard for this species.

Nevertheless, Georgian Bay and its tributaries, including the Moon River to the south, have yielded most of the biggest muskies in North America in the modern era, so there is reason to believe that this wide region has potential for yielding a contender for the all-tackle world-record crown. The muskie angling here is almost exclusively trolling. October is generally considered prime, but the 59-pounder from the French was caught in the summer.

Anglers troll for walleyes in the lower French River. Walleyes and smallmouth bass are the staples in this waterway and are fairly abundant through the season.

THE SOUTHERN
CALIFORNIA ANGLER CAN
HEAD OFFSHORE FROM
SAN DIEGO FOR GOOD
SALTWATER ACTION, OR
INLAND FOR BIG
LARGEMOUTH BASS.

SAN DIEGO
California

San Diego fishermen can boast of the first striped marlin ever taken on a rod and reel, an event that occurred in the Catalina Channel in 1903, and also of having some of the biggest largemouth bass in North America. These are not species that you normally associate with each other, and, of course, the former is in ocean and the latter in freshwater lakes. But that's a combination that exists in few other locales.

Striped marlin are caught as far away as Point Concepcion, but the bulk of activity takes places off San Diego from the Mexican border northward to Catalina and San Clemente Islands and vicinity. Good marlin fishing can be had within 40 miles of San Diego at times. The marlin here are not large. A typical catch might be in the 120- to 150-pound range, with some over 200. The large striped marlin are often caught in these waters early in the season, which extends from July through October, but the best fishing overall is in August and September.

Albacore and yellowtails are caught in some of the same areas, although albacore tend to be further offshore. These are extremely popular off Southern California. The first albacore arrive in late June or early July, and a rush ensues for party and private boat fleets from all ports in the area, lasting until October or November. Although occasionally there are schools of albacore that come to within 20 miles of the coast, most action takes place in the 50- to 100-mile range. Day trips are made at the shorter distances. Yellowtails are caught from April through October and range from 10 to 40 pounds. The main grounds are the Catalina, Channel, and San Clemente islands; the Coronado Islands in Mexico; and from Oceanside to Point Dume along the coast.

Looking inland, the San Diego municipal water-supply lakes, as well as others in the general area (over fifteen), provide some exceptional largemouth bass. Fish over 15 pounds are taken every year, and 20-pounders have been produced. Some think the next world-record largemouth bass will be caught in California; locally, lakes Otay, San Vicente, and Hodges are some of the more notable candidates.

Big boats departing from San Diego take many California anglers to good fishing grounds in nearby and distant offshore environs. Tuna, albacore, and yellowtails are among the prime species sought.

San Diego-area lakes and reservoirs offer some fine bass fishing, with opportunities to catch particularly big largemouths, some twice the size of this specimen.

These are small lakes, however, and the fishing attention is intense, so this is by no means wilderness fishing. On the other hand, the potential is great. Late winter and spring seem to produce the most trophy-size fish, and much fishing is done with light line, fishing deep.

GOUIN RESERVOIR
Quebec

One of the most unusual and rewarding places to fish for both walleyes and northern pike on this continent is Gouin Reservoir in Quebec. Gouin (rhymes with "coin") is a gigantic Canadian lake deep in the wilderness, however it can be reached by car, fishing boat in tow, making it especially desirable to boat-owning anglers and do-it-yourselfers. Yet, despite its accessibility and its fabulous fishing potential, it is known only to a relative handful of North Americans.

Gouin Reservoir is a hydroelectric impoundment that stretches some 65 miles from east to west and 43 miles north to south. It sprawls across the unpaved interior of south-central Quebec. Some anglers access it by float plane, others by vehicle via a four-hour drive over washboard-rutted roads. Traveling to the Barrage (dam) Gouin is an adventure in itself.

A further adventure is navigation on Gouin, which is one of the easiest lakes on the continent to get lost on because of its countless islands, bays, inlets, fingers, and peninsulas

that can get the boater without map, compass, and attentive sense of direction mixed up in a hurry. Nevertheless, there is ample fishing opportunity awaiting, with walleyes and northern pike particularly plentiful.

The walleyes are caught in good average sizes, 2 to 4 pounds, when the spring run is encountered, and by concentrating on some of the major tributaries in late May and early June (such as the Wapous River near Deziel Bay), one can catch plenty of such specimens. Bigger fish, up to 10 pounds, are caught as well, and on the lake proper there is no end to rocky shoals, points, and other desirable walleye locales. The situation is similar with northern pike, although larger sizes are encountered.

Light- to medium-action spinning and bait-casting gear and a good selection of shallow- to deep-running crankbaits and light-to medium-weight jigs, along with a few spoons and spinners, will fill your fishing needs. The lake has deep water, and while it seems to be suitable for trout, apparently none exist here.

GOUIN IS LOCATED DEEP IN THE QUEBEC WOODS, MIDWAY BETWEEN VAL-D'OR AND ROBERVAL AND SOUTH OF CHIBOUGAMOU. IT IS REACHED BY DRIVING FROM TROIS-RIVIERES TO LA TUQUE AND THEN HEADING 125 MILES INLAND.

Submerged timber is indicative of a hydroelectric impoundment and also of the need to navigate carefully, which is true for all areas of the uninhabited and remote Gouin Reservoir. This image was made in a bay near the Wapous River.

A healthy Gouin pike displayed just after capture. Pike and walleyes are the main species here.

A quartet of typical-catch walleyes lies waiting for the fillet knife on the shores of Gouin Reservoir. Walleyes are abundant here and are readily caught through the season.

A campsite overlooks a back bay on Gouin Reservoir. This northern Quebec wilderness impoundment is mammoth, with countless places to explore piscatorially.

LAKE EUFAULA
Alabama/Georgia

LAKE EUFAULA IS ABOUT
A SEVENTY-FIVE-MINUTE
DRIVE SOUTHWEST OF
COLUMBUS, GEORGIA, ON
THE ALABAMA-GEORGIA LINE.

Technically known as Walter F. George Reservoir, and straddling the borders of Alabama and Georgia, Lake Eufaula has been one of the most acclaimed largemouth bass impoundments in North America. In its early years, it was one of the best big bass waters imaginable, and today it has undergone a resurgence that has resulted in classifying it as among the best once again. In addition to having plenty of largemouths, it is also one of the best lakes in the Southeast for catching lunkers, and it possesses a creditable population of hybrid stripers. Additionally, there are many access sites, a national wildlife refuge, and various parks and public-use areas on this lake, befitting its status as one of the more popular places for anglers from throughout the Southeast and Midwest to visit.

There are also many creeks, coves, points, flats, and other good-looking spots to fish along its 640 miles of shoreline, plus a host of not-so-visible structure. And there are crappies, white bass, and other species to catch as well.

Lake Eufaula covers over 45,000 acres. In many places it has tall, red bluff banks, yet it is basically fairly shallow and can produce some very good early-season shallow fishing, especially on newly flooded flats. A few years ago here, during high water, I had some good fishing in newly flooded brush in only a foot of water. But the opposite happens, too. In 1989, authorities drew so much water out of it from late spring and into summer, following the worst flooding on record in the spring, that when I visited in late June 1990 the lake was as shallow as most veteran local anglers had ever seen it, with sandbars and flats clearly exposed in many places. (This, incidentally, made it difficult to get to some locales and also left virtually no water in the backs of some sloughs, creeks, and coves.)

This lake is 85 miles long, so there are numerous places to get to know. The northern sector, above Cowikee Creek, has more riverine features to it, while the southern sector is rather typical of an impoundment environment, with more wide open areas. Eufaula was created in 1963 via a dam on the Chattahoochee River, and it is a major hydroelectric and flood-control reservoir, with the

Fishing dropoffs and ledges are prime locations for procuring largemouth bass. This Eufaula angler is doing just that in a back cove near the Chewalla area.

Springtime anglers work flooded bushes on Lake Eufaula. High water is often experienced here in the early part of the year, and this lake is subject to some extremes in fluctuation, which requires that fishermen adapt accordingly.

result being that almost on a daily basis, current is created along the entire lake when power is being generated or water is being pulled for diversion. Currently a proposal to divert Eufaula to form some of Atlanta's water supply is a hotly contested issue.

For anglers the main diversion, of course, is largemouth bass. The late winter through spring period is especially popular with both local and visiting anglers for producing large bass. It is also a favorable period weather- and temperature-wise, at least in terms of human comfort. However, there are frequently cold fronts that make fishing unpredictable, with the bass success dropping off dramatically until several days of stable conditions prevail. This happens in many southern locales, but is something that northern visiting anglers fail to realize.

Fishing early in the season, especially when the bass are in their spawning mode, is predominantly along shallow flats, espe-

Noted Eufaula angler Larry Columbo lips a nice, and fairly typical, largemouth bass caught late in the day in shallow water.

cially those covered with stumps, brush rows, and vegetation. Many of these are located in the major creeks. Some, however, are in the main lake, in the open-water sections, and extend for great distances. It also takes place along riprap banks (rocky shores, commonly found along dams and bridge roadways). Lipless, sinking crankbaits are a favorite lure here for early in the season, plus shallow-running floating/diving plugs and spinnerbaits.

From the middle to end of spring, the bass start moving to river and creek ledges and deeper water. From then throughout the summer, plastic worms, deep-diving crankbaits, jigging spoons, and tailspinners are preferred, with much reliance on vertical spoon jigging and worm fishing. Using a marker buoy and sonar to search for and pinpoint fish, which are often in a school, is the best tactic.

Hybrid striper fishing kicks into gear in the summer, with good fishing to be had in some locales (often the same daily) early and late in the day. The summer can be brutal on Eufaula, with high heat and humidity, and the midday fishing suffers as a result, in large part due to personal discomfort.

That topwater activity is apparent in the fall, too, from hybrids as well as white bass and also largemouths. The bass move shallower in the fall, and October and November provide good fishing again.

Getting an early start is common at Eufaula, especially in the summer, when the days get very hot. Early and late in the day produces some good striped bass fishing here in the summer and fall.

AWESOME LAKE, ALONG
THE **ENGLISH RIVER**, IS
NORTHEAST OF THE CITY
OF GOOSE BAY, LABRADOR.

*A large speckled trout on
the English River manages
to muster a last burst of
energy before being
subdued. Not visible in
the fray is the large surface
fly in the fish's mouth.*

this province's most beautiful locales, Awesome Lake and the English River have nothing but brook
trout to offer and are virtually un-
known to the international angling
fraternity and, in fact, to most Labra-
dorians. It is within a few hundred
miles of Eagle River and the Minipi
watershed, both of which are renowned in fly-fishing and brook-
trout-angling circles for their
production of outsize fish. But 5- to
8-pounders are a distinct possibility,
if not probability, in the English
River.

Here, there is an untapped bounty
of such fish in river- angling situa-
tions, where the excitement of fly-
fishing with large flies, especially
surface products such as deer-hair
mice, is unmatched. This is a Labrador phenomenon, and one that has
to be seen to be believed. One of the
reasons why large surface flies work
so well, sometimes drifted freely and
sometimes skittered or riffled
across the surface, is because speckled trout here include waterborne
rodents, principally lemmings, as
part of their diet. Having personally
seen several trout with a belly con-
taining one or more of these creatures, I am a believer. And
while mouse imitations work on these fish, such large flies as
a Bomber, Muddler Minnow, and Woolly Worm are also effective.

There are many trout to be had here at certain times,
especially when the season starts in mid- to late June and
through July, and they could readily be caught with hard-
ware, but by choice it has become fly-fishing-only water, with
one trophy over 6 pounds capable of being kept by a guest.

To date, several speckled trout over 8 pounds have been
caught–including a mammoth 28-incher, estimated as weigh-

ENGLISH RIVER
Labrador

The then-unnamed lake that provided a jumpoff point to
anglers fishing the swift runs of the English River in east-central Labrador got the appellation "Awesome Lake" when a
prospective outfitter and his pilot sampled it and came away
stunned with the quality of the speckled (brook) trout fishing
to be had there.

Nestled in the higher country amid mountains in one of

ing at least 9 pounds, which was released. That fish, and many of the other giant speckled trout, have been caught in the English River, which flows out of Awesome Lake. Other good fish are taken seasonally at two or three of the five inlets that come out of the mountains and flow over waterfalls to enter the lake. Awesome Lake is ringed on the west by mountains, including two reaching heights of 3,500 and 3,800 feet, making for an inspiring angling backdrop. Snow remains on the slopes throughout the season. These waters are strictly populated with speckled trout; however, they are not far from the North River, which has some notable sea-run Atlantic salmon.

Well-known angler Len Rich takes a break from his duties as field representative with the Atlantic Salmon Federation to cast a fly for Awesome Lake trout.

Anglers fish an inlet to Awesome Lake for speckled trout, with their tent frame camp in the background. The early part of the season provides good fishing at the several inlets to this lake.

LAKE MICHIGAN IS THE ONLY ONE OF THE GREAT LAKES WHOLLY WITHIN THE UNITED STATES AND IT IS BORDERED BY FOUR STATES.

Steelhead are one of the premier fish of Lake Michigan. This Skamania was taken off Indiana in the summer.

LAKE MICHIGAN
Michigan/Indiana/Wisconsin/Illinois

It's 307 miles long and 118 miles wide at its greatest point. It has a shoreline of over 1,600 miles and sports 22,300 surface acres of water. It is appropriately ranked as a North American fishing hotspot. Some spot, huh?

The "spot" is Lake Michigan. It was the birthplace of the now-heralded modern-day Great Lakes sportfishing restoration effort, which resulted in the stocking of hundreds of millions of fish, the creation of a sportfishing economic impact of over one billion dollars, and the evolution of new tackle, boats, and techniques that advanced sportfishing well beyond the boundaries of its waters.

So how do you encapsulate all of the good things about Lake Michigan into a mere few paragraphs? You don't. Suffice it to note, then, that salmon, trout, bass, walleye, and pike fishing is pretty darned good in lots of areas around this big body of water.

The salmon fishing, while good, has undergone some rough times of late, with a decrease in big fish resulting from a depletion of the alewife and smelt forage base, the very factor that had made the stocking of these Pacific transplants attractive. Nevertheless, the action for these fish, especially in Michigan and Wisconsin waters, is good throughout the season, with particular emphasis on the late summer and early fall fishery. As with other salmon throughout the Great Lakes, fishing is predominantly a trolling (via downrigger) proposition, although fish in the tributaries are caught by wading anglers casting a variety of terminal tackle items.

Trout fishing is good through the spring in shallow water, and later deeper for those who are tuned into searching for these fish. Steelhead fishing is particularly notable, especially off southern Michigan and Indiana in the summer for the highly touted Skamania. This strain

Lake Michigan's rivers and streams support excellent angling for migrating fish. This fall angler is battling a chinook salmon, but fishing for steelhead is also popular, especially through the winter months.

Modern-day big-water trolling tactics got their major development on Lake Michigan as anglers pursued trout, salmon, walleyes, and bass.

of steelhead returns to tributaries in the summer, becoming available in near-shore and shallow environs that would ordinarily be above its temperature range.

Smallmouths, pike, and walleyes are found in various bays, sometimes in notable sizes and sometimes constituting relatively overlooked fisheries. Walleyes, for example, are growing large in Saginaw Bay, and only recently did the general angling public start to focus on this. Some of the catches here are astonishing. Little Bay de Noc is another such place. Most of the fish here are suspended, not hugging bottom, and this has lead to a booming fishery for trollers.

CONTAINING OVER 11,000
SQUARE MILES OF WATER,
GREAT SLAVE LAKE CAN
HARDLY BE MISSED ON
ALMOST ANY MAP. IT IS
ACCESSED BY AIR INTO
YELLOWKNIFE.

*A heavy flow of Snowdrift
River water enters an arm
of Great Slave and gives
this angler cause to cast
for a heavyweight trout.*

GREAT SLAVE LAKE
Northwest Territories

Great Slave Lake is the eleventh-largest lake in the world. It is 298 miles long and in some places over 2,000 feet deep. The eastern region is blessed with islands and peninsulas, which make it geologically distinct from the wide-open remainder of the lake and the prime focus of sportfishing attention. This end has been reserved for sportfishing in recent years, with trophy- fishing regulations in place.

This lake has long been renowned for its lake trout. The laker fishing was best in the mid-1960s, when 40- to 50-pounders were caught (and kept, unfortunately) regularly. Trout grow extremely slowly in this nutrient-poor cold water; 20-pounders are over 20 years old, a 40-pounder may be 50 years old. It takes a long time to replace such fish. Now, rare is the fish that gets kept at the most prominent fishing camp, Frontier Fishing Lodge.

The prospect of catching giant lake trout, however, remains the lake's prime lure. A 74-pounder is reputed to have been netted at Great Slave, and the Frontier camp record stands at 58.5 pounds. This mammoth body of water does contain some monsters.

It also contains plenty of trout that have never seen a lure, and you don't have to be a veteran angler to catch fish. The best trout taken during my last stay there was a deep-bellied 35-pounder caught by a nine-year-old boy.

Trolling near shore around points, reefs, and islands has long been the predominant tactic for lakers here. The water is always cold, and most trout are caught only 10 to 20 feet deep. Large, heavy spoons trolled 100 feet behind the boat are most successfully used, but large plugs will do the job, too. The famous Five of Diamonds spoon—yellow with red-diamond patterns—is a virtual necessity to have and use on this lake, and indeed in most of the large lake trout waters of the Far North.

If catching lakers becomes tedious, you can try your lures on pike. Considering the size of this lake, there are relatively few pike fishing locales. However, these spots—especially Murky Lake--are very good and worth a visit.

Some of the very best angling of all on this lake takes place near the Frontier lodge at the Stark River, using light spinning or fly gear for grayling up to 3 pounds, small pike, and the

Big lake trout are the main draw for Great Slave Lake visitors. Most are caught on large spoons, but some, such as this one, are taken on a plug. Trolling is the main tactic.

The Northwest Territories is truly the Land of the Midnight Sun; this photo was taken near midnight in early August at Great Slave Lake.

occasional whitefish. At the best of times it is a virtual bonanza, and there is good reason to understand why some have called the Stark the greatest grayling river in the world. The possibility of catching 3- to 4-pound fish is also good, and I caught one 3.5-pounder here that was a 2-pound line-class world record for a while.

Anglers who want to use 2- through 8-pound-test lines on spinning gear or 5- to 7-weight fly outfits, can keep busy all week. At times the fishing at the river is remarkably easy. The Stark is shallow, cold, and swift. Pools, eddies, deep holes, and the edges of riffles hold packs of grayling and some lake trout, and the mouth of the river contains a cornucopia of trout, grayling, and whitefish, the latter being a rare catch in general but a possible one here on a small jig or a fly.

A nice plus of fishing here is that one has the opportunity to fish five bodies of water in all: Stark and Snowdrift rivers as well as Stark, Great Slave, and Murky lakes.

Fishing takes place from mid-June through mid-September, with no time that is particularly preferable. The biggest trout appear to be caught in August, though they are deeper. Pike action slows then. Trout spawn at the end of the season, when weather can be harsh, but they move shallower and onto reefs to spawn, so they can be a bit more accessible.

Adding to the value of the fishing, of course, is the landscape, from the mountains that shield Wildbread Bay to the picturesque falls up the Snowdrift River. Particularly impressive, and equally as enjoyable as the fishing, are the spectacular sunsets each evening. I fished until 2:30 in the morning once here, and an orange glow blazed from 10:30 at night until 1:30 as the sun hovered below the horizon. It was just dark enough to make knot tying difficult. By 2 o'clock the sky brightened, and when I stopped fishing a short while later, the sun was up. During midday, when the water is calm, you can see so far across Christie Bay that the world appears to be flat topped. The distant water melts away. Clouds seem to dip halfway into Great Slave Lake. Or does the lake reach up to the clouds? Either way, it is memorable.

Internationally traveled sportsman Paul Merzig displays some nice-size grayling destined for the smokehouse. These fish were caught on flies at the Stark River.

COZUMEL IS LOCATED OFF THE EAST-CENTRAL COAST OF THE YUCATAN PENINSULA.

COZUMEL
Mexico

Cozumel and sailfish are two words that go together in the angler's lexicon. That's because this 33-mile-long island has what may be the most abundant sailfish population in the world. It is an excellent place to do the following: catch sails on light tackle or fly gear; be part of a multiple hookup; achieve a grand slam (white and blue marlin plus sailfish in a single day) or a super grand slam (the other three billfish plus swordfish).

Sailfish are most abundant from February to June, but can be caught at all times. A slow day off Cozumel, three or four sailfish, is a good day almost anywhere else. Dolphin, kingfish, bonito, and blackfin tuna are also in the offshore mixed bag, sometimes in good numbers and sizes, although they are usually an incidental catch while going after billfish.

Trolling at Cozumel predominantly takes place between the island and the mainland, often close to the Yucatan near Playa del Carmen in 10 to 60 fathoms of water. Sailfish migrate northward with the strong current, coming from the open waters of the Caribbean and working their way up the coast past Cozumel, passing the head of the peninsula at Isla Mujeres and Cancun, and then moving into the Gulf of Mexico. Some Cozumel boats run north toward Isla Mujeres later in the season, when the main run of sailfish is more clustered up there.

White marlin are sometimes caught in the same locales as sailfish. Blue marlin are usually caught further offshore and over deeper water, usually while fishing larger baits or lures

Sailfish are plentiful in the waters off Cozumel and all along the coast in that region of Mexico. This one leaps and twists in its bid for freedom.

than would be used for the other billfish. Swordfish are occasionally spotted finning along the surface here, and there is a slight chance of hooking one by casting a live bait to a sighted broadbill or by fishing at night. Trolling with bait is the primary technique for sails, and some live bait fishing is done.

Although bonefish are abundant along the Yucatan flats on the mainland, they are not as abundant at Cozumel because the island has little shallow water. There are some bonefish and permit to be caught here, however, in lagoons at either end of the island, and these are well worth exploring. The fish aren't big in either locale, but the setting is pristine and tranquil.

Very little attention has been devoted to reef fishing here, although the reefs around Cozumel are rated as among the world's finest for diving. Palancar Reef, which surrounds Cozumel, is the world's second-largest coral reef. The edges yield groupers and red snapper and the occasional dolphin, kingfish, and amberjack.

This bonefish was taken in a lagoon near the tip of the island. Cozumel supports offshore, reef, and limited inshore fishing.

LOCATED IN CENTRAL NEW HAMPSHIRE, **SQUAM LAKE** IS REACHED BY TAKING I-93 TO ASHLAND, THEN U.S. 3 EAST TO HOLDERNESS.

Landlocked salmon and lake trout, the latter being netted here at Cotton Cove, are favorites of local anglers, especially in the spring.

SQUAM LAKE
New Hampshire

If you've seen the movie *On Golden Pond*, then you've seen Squam Lake. That memorable, poignant film was shot on location at this attractive site. Remember the cry of the loons and the sunsets? Remember Purgatory Cove, actually known as Kimball Island? Remember Fred, Henry Fonda's long-sought lunker rainbow trout that lived in the pond? That trout was a Hollywood conception, although there are some lake trout (deep and tough to come by most of the year) here.

It is actually the smallmouth bass for which this lovely lake

in the foothills of New Hampshire's White Mountains is justly noted among anglers. A few years ago, the results of a fish-and-game survey of Squam indicated that it had a tremendous population of smallmouths, perhaps the best in the state according to officials at the time. In addition to that, it has some fine landlocked salmon angling, including larger-on-average size landlocks than its bigger, nearby sister lake, Winnipesaukee.

Squam, at 6,764 acres, is the second-largest lake in New Hampshire. It is a predominantly deep body of water, with plenty of islands and rocky shoals. The water is pure and crystal clear, and you can watch a jig drift off to the bottom

in depths twice your body length and then some. It is so clear that in the spring you may even be able to see smallmouths attack your lures.

The finest time for smallmouth fishing is in the spring, from early June through the fourth of July. Once the weather sets in and the surface layers warm up, bass go deep and retreat to the areas around deep, rocky shoals. Some great fishing can be had at Squam in midsummer, if you locate these spots and work them carefully, using jigs, live crayfish, and perhaps surface plugs in the evening.

For landlocked salmon, the months of April and May, when the fish are closer to the surface and near shore in pursuit of spawning smelt, are the best times to fish. There is little nonfishing boat traffic at that time and plenty of salmon to be had. Most anglers here fish traditionally, trolling streamer flies on a fly line or lead core line. Later, the fish will move deeper and be harder to locate.

That is also a good time to be fishing for smaller species. White perch are particularly large in this lake. My ex-brother-in-law caught and ate one once that would have been a state record.

Picturesque Squam Lake is one of New England's finest smallmouth bass waters, with plenty of rocky shoals and islands around which bass congregate.

NOVA SCOTIA, WHICH
BORDERS NEW BRUNSWICK,
IS SEPARATED FROM THE
MAINLAND UNITED STATES
BY THE BAY OF FUNDY.

NOVA SCOTIA

To a sport fisherman this small province is the premier domain of two of the world's greatest gamefish: bluefin tuna and Atlantic salmon.

The cold Atlantic waters off the mainland and Cape Breton Island are grounds for the true giant bluefin tuna. A "giant" might be a 500- or 800-pounder farther south, but here it is 1,000 pounds or more, and this is where you go if you want the best chance of battling such a fish on rod and reel. The province's best such catch was a 1,496-pounder, caught in St. Georges Bay. This action takes place in late summer and early fall, when the fish arrive in their migratory cycle.

Salmon, too, are a migrant here, with fishing concentrated in freshwater environs in numerous flowages. Although there are many salmon rivers in the province, the premier ones include the La Have, Margaree, St. Mary's, Gold, Stewiacke,

and Medway rivers. The Margaree may be the best known of these, but the La Have is currently the best-producing water. Some salmon are available in late June, but the better concentrations are from mid-July through September.

Nova Scotia also has some other remarkably good, and grossly overlooked, freshwater angling. Shad run many of the coastal rivers and are extremely abundant in some, especially the Annapolis and Gaspereau systems, in May and early June. Smallmouth bass are found in a host of lakes and reservoirs, especially in the vicinity of New Minas, and most of these don't see much angling all season long. Both of these fish are abundant, with plenty of opportunity to be caught on fly-rod presentations.

A fly-fisherman works the tail of a pool for Atlantic salmon on the La Have River.

OTTAWA RIVER
Ontario

She's a big river, the Ottawa, hundreds of miles long and forming a border between the provinces of Ontario and Quebec. But in the wild, remote-but-accessible Upper Ottawa Valley, she is loaded with good fishing opportunities, in a setting that is appreciated by many anglers season after season.

The foremost draw for these anglers is walleye, and on the Ottawa there is no better time for fast action than when the provincial season opener occurs on the second Saturday of May. The standard catch is in the 2- and 3-pound range, but some trophies in the 8- to 10-pound class are found in this section of river.

Also found is a plentiful supply of northern pike, plus smallmouth bass. There are no muskies here, but surprisingly there are a lot of largemouths in backwater locales, and these cover-seeking fish are virtually overlooked by all the folks concentrating on walleyes and smallmouths in the main flowage.

Besides having enjoyable fishing on the Ottawa, the visitors will notice that there is not a big crowd to share it with; that there is opportunity to get away and explore a bit (a few back bays and meandering creeks lead to notable hideaways with good fishing); and that one watches the water closely while navigating, as this area is used for log transportation and floating booms, and log-collection points exist.

Two anglers work a backwater bay off the Ottawa River for largemouth bass and pike. The main-river water is noted for its walleyes and smallmouth bass.

THE AREA FROM MATTAWA TO SOUTH OF PEMBROKE A FEW MILES IS ONE OF THE BETTER LOCALES ON THE **OTTAWA RIVER**.

KENTUCKY AND BARKLEY LAKES STRADDLE THE WESTERN KENTUCKY-TENNESSEE BORDER AND ARE ENVELOPED BY LAND BETWEEN THE LAKES, A NATIONAL RECREATION AREA MANAGED BY THE TVA.

Smallmouth bass, like the one being held by this evening angler, and largemouth bass are abundant in Kentucky and Barkley lakes.

KENTUCKY AND BARKLEY LAKES
Kentucky/Tennessee

When they say that Kentucky and Barkley lakes contain millions of fish, they aren't kidding. Kentucky and Barkley lakes also have a lot of water. Some 3,500 miles of shoreline, 220,000 surface acres, and a status as the second-largest manmade water system in North America constitute one whale of a place to go fishing.

There are countless coves, bays, fingers, and hideaways for bass and crappie fishing here. Barkley is the smaller of the two lakes, and the younger by twenty years, and is connected by a navigable canal. Where Barkley has an average depth of 10 feet, Kentucky has an average of 14, with more gravel areas and slightly less siltation. That relative clarity may have been the key to the establishment of smallmouth bass, which have done well in the last decade.

Barkley's bass catch has historically been almost entirely largemouths. Kentucky's largemouths have been plentiful, and there are a lot of spotted bass in the lake as well. Though there is a lot of shoreline fishing, many bass are caught around submerged islands as well.

Current plays a big role in successful fishing here, too. Kentucky and Barkley are not your typical standing bodies of water. They don't stratify thermally, and they pass a lot of water from the Tennessee River to the Ohio River. Fishing the downstream side of points and other areas where current affects feeding and food availability can be an important factor.

Great numbers of bass are caught in the summertime because of the number of people on the lakes, but the better action is found in spring, fall, and late winter. A warm spell in February or March can turn the bass on, though, and that fishing can be good until the crappies spawn. The bass spawn in May and late May through June are also good fishing times. Although giant bass, 10 pounds or more, are rare, 6- to 8-pounders are available, plus good numbers of intermediate-size fish.Crappies are available throughout the season, but are most heavily pursued in the spring. A particularly good site then is the creeks entering the Big Sandy River area. Some 150 fish-attractor sites (brushpiles) have been constructed by the Tennessee Valley Authority (TVA), incidentally, and these are very popular fishing locales. Crappie fishing here is as big an undertaking as is bass fishing, and many local guides specialize in it.

Fishermen work a deep spot with jigs for crappies. Kentucky and Barkley lakes are among the most noted crappie waters of North America.

THE GRAND-SLAM FISHING
OF WESTERN LABRADOR
IS ACCESSED FROM WABUSH/
LABRADOR CITY, NEAR
THE BORDER OF QUEBEC,
VIA A ONE- TO TWO-HOUR
FLOAT-PLANE RIDE.

Anglers and their guide troll in a protected deep-water bay for lake trout, with the Ashuanipi River in the background. Cool, spring-fed bays provide good laker action late in the season.

ASHUANIPI RIVER
Labrador

The Ashuanipi River of western Labrador is part of the massive watershed that encompasses Smallwood Reservoir. As the locals say, there is "a lot of water" here, and this includes a major river as well as countless backwater expanses that were created years ago when the water was backed up by a dam.

This watershed has been known for its production of ouananiche, or landlocked Atlantic salmon, partly because it has produced the world record for this species, but the area is surely Labrador's most noteworthy multifaceted fishery. Salmon, speckled (brook) trout, lake trout, splake, northern pike, and whitefish beckon sportsmen, making it an attraction for anglers from throughout North America who have a diversity of interests.

Accessed only by float plane and primarily from Wabush/Labrador City, this region sees few visitors each year, and then only from late June through early September.

The better fishing for landlocked salmon occurs in June and again in late August and September, as there are two runs (seems unusual but true) of salmon. Smaller fish are possible in the rivers, especially in the pools and quick water between lakes, all summer long, being caught on spinners, spoons, and flies.

The speckled trout here are plentiful in certain places and can be had up to 7 pounds. Some sections of this area rival the better-known brook trout waters in the eastern part of this province, and 4- and 5-pounders are regularly caught. The Ashuanipi and McKenzie rivers produce many trout in the 3- to 5-pound class, which is outstanding by any standards, plus the occasional larger fish. Murray River and the outflow of Crossroads Lake are also very good, and undoubtedly many locales produce great results at certain times, especially if the water is not too low. Speckled trout can be caught all season long and on various lures. The bigger fish are particularly fond of surface flies, especially Bombers and mouse (actually lemming) imitations, which makes for some really exciting moments.

Lakers here have been caught in excess of 20 pounds, but these are rather rare. Four- to 8-pounders are more likely, with some fish in the 10- or 12-pound class as well. In some places you can catch lakers one right after the other. Pike are similar; few really large ones are caught with any regularity, but there is a good supply of smaller fish, though not much in the way of traditional weed bed fishing. *Splake*, which are a natural cross between lake and brook trout, occur in certain systems, and whitefish are plentiful enough to be caught on spinners and plugs while fishing for other species.

Several rivers in this region, such as the outlet of Crossroads Lake shown here, provide excellent action for speckled trout, with the possibility of big fish and salmon as well.

Catching fresh fish for a shore lunch is no problem on the Ashuanipi River. In some places, such as this rapids, the species could include lake trout, speckled trout, ouananiche (landlocked salmon), or possibly pike.

TO REACH **LAKE OF THE WOODS** BY AUTO, DRIVE TO BAUDETTE, WARROAD, OR NORTHWEST ANGLE IN MINNESOTA, OR MORSON, NESTOR FALLS, SIOUX NARROWS, OR KENORA IN ONTARIO.

A large smallmouth bass comes to net on Lake of the Woods. Smallmouths and walleyes are the most highly sought sportfish in this lake and are abundant in many areas.

LAKE OF THE WOODS
Minnesota

Lake of the Woods has the size and fish that befit its status as the preeminent north-central warm-water fishery of North America. It is roughly 66 miles long (from Baudette, Minnesota, to Kenora, Ontario) and 52 miles wide (from Northwest Angle, Minnesota, to Nestor Falls, Ontario). There are over 14,000 islands on Lake of the Woods—most are in Canadian water—and to say that one can get lost quite easily, or spend a lot of time searching for fishing hotspots, is an understatement.

This is truly a picture-postcard lake, characterized by rocky shores, some weedy bays, and a hearty shoreline mixture of conifers and hardwoods. Its rough-woods wilderness profile is only occasionally punctuated by houses, camps, or boat docks, and you can travel in some portions of the lake without seeing any signs of civilization. The center and northern sectors house nearly all of the islands. The wide-open southern expanse of Big Traverse Bay is in Minnesota; it is fairly shallow, with few reefs and islands, and does not offer the extensive angling found from the Ontario border northward.

The angling here is among the best to be found in North America for several species of fish, most notably smallmouth bass, walleye, pike, and muskie.

The bass don't tend to run particularly large; there are jillions of them, and the average size is in the 2-pound-or-just-under range. The best smallmouth fishing is found in the central portion and northern half of the lake. Most angling is in relatively shallow water throughout the season. The hottest action occurs when the bass are on the spawning beds in shallow water close to shore, which usually occurs in mid-June. A cold winter giving way to late spring can delay this by a week or more, but even if warm weather comes late, by the end of June and early July expect some explosive shallow-water surface action.

Jigs are the main ticket for smallies, but spinners, some crankbaits, and surface plugs are useful. Largemouth bass are present here, too, but greatly outnumbered by their

A Lake of the Woods smallmouth provides explosive action for these springtime anglers. Shallow bays and coves produce the best bass opportunities early in the season.

If you're walleye fishing regularly, you'll surely catch a few northern pike; while jigging you'll undoubtedly be cut off a few times each day as well. If you pursue pike expressly, you'll find plenty. Leader-linked lures—such as spinners, spinnerbaits, spoons, and some muskie plugs—will catch pike in their favored, weedy haunts, though the bigger fish seem to be off rocky points or reefs. Four-to 5-pounders are common, and there are opportunities for much larger ones, including the occasional pike in the 18- to 25-pound range.

The muskie population is extraordinary, and Lake of the Woods is surely the hands-down best water in North America for having a good chance of catching a fish 30 pounds or better. The average size is about 18 pounds, but a *lot* of 20- to 30-pounders are caught (many released) annually. The muskie season opens in mid-June and is good through the fall. August may be the best month; the fish are very active and shallow and will even strike surface lures. Bucktail spinners are the foremost muskie lure here, followed by jerkbaits, swimming plugs, and crankbaits. This is almost entirely a casting fishery with little opportunity for trolling. Shallow water, rocky reefs, and submerged weed growth are everywhere.

Early in the summer, muskies are found in the same locales as walleyes, which are their primary forage. By midsummer they have moved onto reefs with good weed cover. The midsection of the lake, from Monument Bay to Sabaskosing Bay, is prime muskie territory, and there's a lot of territory to cover.

Lake of the Woods is a sportsman's paradise. On a calm night, when a thin cloud veils a setting orange sun, and a loon cries just after you've boated yet another walleye, you'll have an indescribably satisfied feeling. It's what a fisherman's dreams are made of.

The view from Centre Island makes Lake of the Woods look like a small place, but indeed, these are just islands in the middle of a huge, scenic body of water.

cousins and mostly found in the northern area closer to Kenora.

Walleyes are plentiful as well, with the possibility of getting some in the 7-pound-and-up class. Walleyes get a lot of attention here in mid-May, when the season opens and the fishing is fast and relatively easy.

The mayfly hatch of late spring and early summer drops walleye fishing success for a while, as the fish feed heavily on this bountiful protein. They then leave the bays and head for rocky reefs and, to a lesser degree, deep-water points and rocky islands. In summer you can either run from one reef to another until you find a locale with a school of active, feeding fish on top of it (usually in just 5 to 6 feet of water) or stay on one reef for a long time, waiting for the fish to come in to feed. Near the end of summer the walleyes leave the reefs, moving into weedy bays that have mud and sand bottoms, where they feed primarily on yellow perch.

A small muskellunge froths the water for a successful angler. Lake of the Woods is the continent's premier muskie fishing lake, and the summer through fall period is outstanding for these fish.

THE **SEA OF CORTEZ**
IS A GULF SITUATED
BETWEEN BAJA PENINSULA
AND THE WESTERN
MEXICAN MAINLAND.

*These sailfish didn't wash
ashore, but they are
dutifully admired by
Mexican villagers when
sportfishermen return with
the catch.*

SEA OF CORTEZ
Mexico

The interior section of the Sea of Cortez, which is actually the Gulf of California, has an abundant and diverse fishery for its near-600-mile length. The coastline throughout the Sea of Cortez is probably a thousand miles long, with a vast amount of uninhabited area and sections that seldom get fished. With all the places to explore and all the species to be had, it is no wonder that many visiting anglers use a lot of superlatives to describe it.

The Sea of Cortez abounds with fish, but also with rocky shores and cliffs, islands, inlets, beaches, and diverse habitats that appeals to those fish. Some of these are located at or near the more accessible locales, such as Loreto, Mulege, and Santa Rosalia in Baja California Sur; Bahia de Los Angeles, Puertocitos, and San Felipe to the north in Baja California; and Puerto Penasco, El Desemboque, Puerto Lobos, and Bahia Kino along the eastern mainland. Migratory species tend to be more concentrated in the southern half of the Sea of Cortez, with its deeper water and greater current influence.

From Kino Bay on the west to Loreto on the east, the striped marlin and sailfish are generally less plentiful, but the light-tackle angling for other species can rate with the best anywhere.

Roosterfish and jack crevalle, both of which are extremely hard fighters, are among the more popular gamefish in the Sea of Cortez, and they are found in various locales. Dolphin, or dorado, are also a favorite target. They range well into the gulf, up through the middle islands, but are more abundant in the southern half of the Cortez. Trolling with lures or fishing live bait is standard.

Striped marlin and sailfish are a possibility along Baja California Sur from Loreto to La Paz, but the best opportunities exist from La Paz southward. Sailfish, which are likely to venture closer to shore and in slightly warmer water, are found from Loreto to La Paz. The area near Loreto, with its chain of uninhabited offshore islands, especially Carmen and Coronado, is the best bet in the interior gulf for a chance at migratory yellowfin tuna and also a good spot for yellowtail.

Yellowtail migrate northward to the middle of the Cortez, almost to the upper third. The islands in the upper Gulf, including Tiburon near Kino Bay, provide good fishing from late spring through summer. Bonito are caught here and throughout the Cortez, moving out of the northern reaches with cooler fall weather.

Summer is a good time to be fishing the Sea of Cortez for virtually all species, despite the fact that it is very hot then. The warmer waters are especially favored by the migratory fish, including billfish (which are less abundant the further north you go) and dolphin.

The author plays a sailfish that chooses to show its acrobatic talents close to the boat. Billfish and other migratory species are prime attractions for Sea of Cortez anglers.

GREAT BEAR LAKE
SPRAWLS OVER THE
ARCTIC CIRCLE WITH FIVE
MAJOR ARMS REACHING
IN ALL DIRECTIONS.

*The Coppermine River,
shown here, and the Tree
River, are favored locales
for fly-out expeditions from
Great Bear Lake by anglers
in search of arctic char.*

GREAT BEAR LAKE
Northwest Territories

There is no locale that is known more widely for lake trout than Canada's Northwest Territories, although calling this province a "locale" is about as preposterous as calling its most famous body of water a lake. Considering its stature as the eighth-largest freshwater lake in the world, Great Bear Lake might be more appropriately called the Great Bear Sea, or, better yet, Great Trout Sea.

Great Bear is actually the fourth-largest lake in North America, ranking behind lakes Superior, Huron, and Mich-igan in size. When you consider that it has an infinitesi-mally small percentage of the boat traffic and fishing pressure of those other large North American lakes, and that it is so remote that it straddles the Arctic Circle, you can comprehend the allure it has as a distant fishing locale, especially for American lake trout aficionados.

The big draw is the fact that this mammoth water is responsible for six of the nine current line-class world-record lakers, ranging from 49 to 63 pounds, all set in the last decade, plus one fly rod record, and, of course, the gran-daddy of them all, the 65-pound all-tackle world-record lake trout, caught on August 8, 1970.

Does another all-tackle record swim here? It's almost a certainty. But will anyone ever catch it? You would think that as old as these monsters are here—virtually as old as they are heavy—that they didn't get this way by being gullible. And yet, the tried-and-true method of lake trout fishing here, trolling with the biggest spoons and plugs, is the technique that works day after day, week after week, and season after season.

The big lakers come at all times of the summer, too, though some regulars prefer early in the summer to get the ice-out advantage while others prefer late in the summer when the fish are heavier and ready to spawn.

That's not the only fishing available, however. The lake is also known for big grayling. Four of six line-class world records, plus the all-tackle world record (5 pounds, 15 ounces), were established here. Great Bear anglers also get in some mighty fine arctic char fishing on the Tree and Coppermine rivers, via fly-outs from main lodges. These rivers have been known to produce really big char, from 15 to 22 pounds, plus the all-tackle world record, a 32-pounder taken in 1981.

It is said that because of its enormous size, Great Bear Lake has some places that have never been fished. For sure, there is a lot of water to cover for anglers who spend just a week there.

Good-size lake trout and shore lunches are characteristic of fishing experiences in the Northwest Territories.

SANTEE-COOPER IS BISECTED BY THE MAJOR NORTH-SOUTH ARTERY I-95. FROM COLUMBIA, IT IS REACHED BY TAKING I-26 TO U.S. 301.

The early and late hours of the day provide notable moments at Santee-Cooper, especially in summer and fall.

Striped bass have generated a lot of excitement at Santee-Cooper, and the fish from here have been used to initiate striper-stocking programs all over the United States. This one is about average in size, but much larger fish are present.

This 25-pound catfish is big by most standards, but at Santee-Cooper these fish come in much larger sizes, especially in the Diversion Canal, where this photo was taken.

SANTEE-COOPER
South Carolina

When the Santee and Cooper rivers in South Carolina were dammed in 1941, striped bass migrating from the ocean were trapped in newly formed lakes Marion and Moultrie. Thus was born the phenomenon of inland striped bass fishing. From this stock of fish over thirty states ultimately received stripers to plant in impoundments that were full of baitfish and had suitable deep, open-water habitat.

These two lakes, known collectively as Santee-Cooper, were to undergo a phenomenal new-lake boom, and ultimately 30- to 50-pound linesides would be taken at the same time that 10-pound largemouths were gracing the boats of other anglers. It was quite a fishery in the growth years. Today, after a stabilization period in which largemouths seemed to suffer and giant striped bass disappeared, both species are again prospering. There is a very vital fishery for both, and they are vigorously pursued by local and visiting anglers each year.

The better striped bass fishing occurs in the spring and

fall. In spring, the fish run up the rivers to spawn, and in the main lake situate themselves in areas with significant current. Summer fishing is not especially productive; stripers move deep and are harder to locate and catch, though some anglers troll the old river channels with success.

The most dynamic striper fishing at Santee-Cooper occurs later in the year when schooling fish mass and attack shad. This begins in late summer with small stripers and continues in earnest from fall through winter, when bigger stripers pick up the pace. All manner of lead-head jigs, jigging spoons, lead-bodied lures, and popping plugs or stickbaits will catch surface-schooling fish. Angling is frenzied as boats race to the fish, which are sometimes located by looking for seagulls working the commotion for scraps.

Largemouth bass enthusiasts continue to find success in the Santee-Cooper lakes, too. There aren't as many 8- to 10-pounders as in years past, but there are still a lot of big fish and plenty of small- and intermediate-size ones. Santee-Cooper is predominantly shallow, with good cover and spawning habitat for bass close to the surface. With over 170,000 acres of water between the two lakes, there are a lot of old swamps and backwater ponds that seem to be especially attractive to roving largemouth bass. Fishing for largemouths, like stripers, is best in spring and fall, and poorest during the summer heat. Plastic worms, spinnerbaits, crankbaits, and

surface lures all have merit, but worms and spinnerbaits fished around wood and vegetation are the prominent lures. Tackle needs to be fairly stiff, with relatively heavy line. There is a lot of cover in these lakes, especially Marion, and that includes standing dead timber, live cypress trees, and stumps.

Santee-Cooper also hosts a great population of catfish, including blues, channels, and flatheads. Some of these reach

Lakes Marion and Moultrie have provided some exceptionally good largemouth bass fishing since they were created and the timber on the land was flooded.

monstrous proportions, and no doubt Santee-Cooper is one of the top two or three spots in North America for a chance at catching a catfish that is 20 pounds or better. This is almost entirely a matter of stillfishing or drifting along the bottom using dead bait, primarily chunked herring. The Diversion Canal between the lakes, which has current, is one of the better big cat locales.

ALAGNAK RIVER
Alaska

There are a lot of great places to fish in Alaska, but you'd be hard-pressed to beat the experiences to be enjoyed on the Alagnak River, south of Lake Iliamna. This wild and scenic river is part of the Bristol Bay watershed and loaded with trout, salmon, and grayling, with opportunities for large fish and angling with fly rod as well as conventional tackle.

Rainbow trout and king (chinook) salmon are the prime attractions, but excellent fishing is enjoyed here for sockeye salmon and silvers (cohos) as well. The time of the season depends a lot on availability.

Kings appear in early June and are present until early August, with the last three weeks of July being prime for trophy fish, including those in the 30- to 60-pound range. Sockeye and chum salmon are migrating by at the same time, and it is possible to wear yourself out catching the energetic sockeye, with a couple dozen a day possible on a fly.

Lots of action on silver salmon follows in August and September, with the average size of these acrobatic fish being 8 to 12 pounds and some specimens weighing up to 20. Rainbow trout fishing is especially good at this time also, and the Alagnak hosts some 12-to 20-pound brutes, which are a handful on a fly rod. Additionally, the river hosts grayling, Dolly Varden, and northern pike.

All of these fish are great battlers, and the salmon in particular are charged, as they are fresh from the salt here.

THE **ALAGNAK RIVER** IS ON THE ALASKAN PENINSULA, DRAINING OUT OF KATMAI NATIONAL PARK.

Big king, or chinook, salmon are found in the Alagnak River, as well as many other species of fish, giving it a diversity that is especially appealing.

THE BASS WATERS OF SOUTHWESTERN NEW BRUNSWICK ARE JUST A SHORT DISTANCE FROM EASTERN MAINE, WITH SOME OF THEM ACTUALLY ON THE BORDER. THEY ARE READILY ACCESSIBLE BY AUTO AND BY AIR FROM FREDERICTON.

SOUTHWESTERN NEW BRUNSWICK

Although bass are far from endangered, there's no doubt that intense interest, publicity, and angling pressure have resulted in tough fishing in some places. I've seen this, and heard about it, from people in Oklahoma, Georgia, Ohio, California, and elsewhere in North America. Recently, an Alabama friend—who is an accomplished longtime bass fisherman and a former competitive angler—told me that compared to what he used to experience, today's new crop of fishermen don't know what "good" really is.

Well, here's a place where the bass fishing is *really* good by any standards. The pressure is light, as local anglers generally ignore bass in preference to salmon, and there are varied waters to try. It is more than enough to provide an antidote for any bass aficionado suffering from a lack of action, and those who want to experience some of the best smallmouth angling anywhere need not look much further. The place—better known for its Atlantic salmon fishery, trophy whitetail deer, black bears, thick woods, and bugs—is the southwestern corner of the Canadian Maritime Province of New Brunswick.

The most obvious of New Brunswick's smallmouth bass waters is the massive (60-mile-long) lake just north of the capital city of Fredericton, locally called the Mactaquac Headpond. This is a twenty-two-year-old impoundment of the St. John River, and it has plentiful, and large, smallmouths.

Most of the dozens of other rock- and boulder-laden smallmouth lakes in southwestern New Brunswick are easy to find and cool enough to provide good angling through the summer. Some of the more notable ones include Harvey, Oromocto, East Grand, Little Magaguadivic, and George. They're places that you can fish with a guide or on

your own (if the latter, be extremely careful, as some are tricky to navigate), and they hold enough bass so you can have reasonable success even when angling conditions aren't prime.

There is some good river fishing to be had as well, one of the most notable being the Meduxnekeag River from Jackson Falls to Woodstock (which also has nice brown trout).

A wide range of tackle choices make fishing suitable to anglers of all interest here, with fly and spinning gear of most merit, especially in the early part of the season. Surface lures and spinnerbaits are very effective, and a jig fisherman will find that most smallmouths here have not yet discovered what these wonderful little lures are.

A nice smallmouth bass is landed on the Meduxnekeag River of New Brunswick. Good brown trout and smallmouth bass action can be enjoyed here on the same float trip.

George Lake produced a smallmouth doubleheader for these anglers. A number of lakes scattered around southwestern New Brunswick provide smallmouth bass fishing that is among the best in North America.

In addition to supplying excellent bass fishing in lakes, southwestern New Brunswick also offers opportunities to view wildlife—including black bears and whitetail deer—as well as rivers teeming with brown trout.

131

SAM RAYBURN IS NEAR LUFKIN, TEXAS, AND CAN BE REACHED BY TAKING U.S. 69, 59, OR 96.

LAKE SAM RAYBURN
Texas

At 114,000 acres, Lake Sam Rayburn in east Texas dwarfs many of the other well-known bass waters of the United States. Like many impoundments, it has gone through a boom-bust cycle of fish populations and was written off by many people little more than ten years ago. But today, there are enough all-season angling opportunities here, especially for the highly revered (in Texas) largemouth bass, to qualify it as a premier lake. What primarily attracts people to this lake is bass of all sizes. There are plenty of 3- and 4-pound largemouths in the lake, with a good number of 5- to 8-pounders.

One of the things that contributed to a new era of bass angling at Sam Rayburn was a drought and a drawdown of the lake in the early 1980s. That spurred the growth of new, near-shore cover that helped create new habitat for baitfish and bass. Another thing has been the growth of coontail moss, pond weed, and hydrilla, which provide cover and feeding opportunities as well as identifiable places to fish.

With 560 miles of shoreline and over 45 miles of water between the north and south ends, Sam Rayburn indeed has a lot of water to fish. As with most big impoundments, creeks, submerged creek channels, the back ends of coves and bays, and the flats and dropoffs adjacent to deep water offer good places for anglers to direct their beginning efforts.

Bass normally spawn here in March and April, sometimes in stages, with shallower coves and southerly creeks warming up faster than other locations. However, some of the lake's best fishing is experienced in late February and early March, when bass are active and moving into staging areas to spawn. Late-winter weather, however, can be quite unpredictable.

The best early-season angling for big prespawn fish takes place in the creeks and on the edges of creek channels. Places like Coleman Creek, Ayish Bayou, Buck Bay, and Five Fingers to the south, and the creeks off the Angelina and Atoyac Arms to the north, attract attention. The deeper edges of the creek channels produce late in the year, and the vegetation is particularly worth fishing during the late spring and summer months.

Sam Rayburn is heavily timbered in many areas, especially in the creeks, with a lot of submerged trees and stumps. Fairly heavy line is the rule here. Jigs, adorned with pork or eel chunks, are especially favored, both for flipping and casting. Plastic worms and jigging spoons catch fish, too, as do spinnerbaits and surface lures.

A bass boat, a standard sight on Sam Rayburn, races across the water to another prospective largemouth hole.

Vegetation at Sam Rayburn has proved a boon to largemouth bass, which are the premier quarry at this large, manmade lake.

LOCATED 250 MILES
NORTH OF THE ARCTIC
CIRCLE AT THE
SEVENTIETH PARALLEL,
VICTORIA ISLAND IS
ACCESSED BY AIR FROM
YELLOWKNIFE TO
CAMBRIDGE BAY.

*Victoria Island is world
renowned for its arctic
char. A world-record
specimen, weighing in at
24 pounds, was caught
here in 1982. Fishermen
also make pilgrimages
here to take advantage of
exceptional lake trout
opportunities.*

VICTORIA ISLAND
Northwest Territories

The moment that you step off the commercial airliner at
Cambridge Bay you realize that Victoria Island is a special
place. Across from the airport is a Distant Early Warning
(DEW) radar site. In the bay is the wreck of the *Maud*, the
round-hulled vessel used by Norwegian explorer Roald
Amundsen to make the first east-west crossing of the Canadian Arctic at the turn of this century. A few yards from that
is the site of the first church here, a Roman Catholic building
made of double stone walls, with caribou hides for insulation.
Perhaps a visit will coincide with the biggest event of the
season, the arrival of the supply barge that is laden with
goods ordered a year earlier, whose passage is cleared by
icebreakers. In Cambridge Bay, drying char and animal skins
hang outside houses. Dog sleds lie next to all-terrain vehicles
(ATVs) and snowmobiles.

Located above the mainland Northwest Territories, north
of the Arctic Circle and in the lower reaches of the Arctic
Ocean, Victoria Island is a *long* way from anywhere. It's a
particularly long way to go to stand waist-deep in a river that
never gets warmer than 40 degrees F, under a gray, sometimes drizzly or snowy sky, and cast for a fish that may not
be there. Much of the time there is only the whistling of wind
for company or an occasional caribou a half mile away on the
horizon. Other than caribou, musk oxen, and rocks, there is
nothing here that rises more than a few inches off the ground.
The nearest tree is 400 miles to the south, across a spongy,
moss-covered, nearly level plain that hides an always-frozen
substrata.

But in this apparently desolate spot are treasures that only
several dozen fishermen are able to enjoy each summer. In
some of Victoria Island's rivers, which flow north to the
Viscount Melville Sound and south to the Coronation and
Queen Maud gulfs, not far from the permanent polar icecap,
the lucky ones will intercept the elusive, brilliantly colored
arctic char on the way to its spawning grounds. For this is
probably the premier spot in all of North America for having
a chance at catching a trophy-size member of a coveted,
hard-fighting, and elusive species that few people ever see in
person.

Certainly, arctic char, *Salvelinus alpinus,* are found all across the North American Arctic. The largest char appear to come regularly from Victoria Island and the Tree River on the mainland Northwest Territories. Geographically, these places are not that far apart, yet their char are distinctly different. Tree River char in their spawning colors have a dark back and are not fully swathed in red or orange. They have a humped back, too, and often a more pronounced kype. Many taxidermists, more familiar with these trophies, have painted this pattern on Victoria Island trophies.

The biggest char caught at Victoria Island's only fishing camp, High Arctic Lodge, was a line-class world-record 24-pounder taken in 1982. Several other line-class world records have been established here as well. Summer char here typically run from 12 to 20 pounds, a weight well above that found in most other regions.

Char spawn approximately every three years, and it is the spawning fish that change colors and are largest and most prized. Silver char, those descending lakes and rivers and running out to the ocean for the summer, are smaller and bright, though a lot of fun to catch. Fishing is done for silver

char in July and holdover (spawning) char in August. The season, which is just six weeks long, begins in mid-July and runs through August, by which time the weather is already starting to get worrisome.

In addition to having tremendous char fishing, Victoria Island has some exceptional lake trout angling. Lakers up to 44 pounds have been caught in relatively shallow 15-mile-long Merkley Lake, site of the base camp for High Arctic Lodge. In fact, some anglers venture all this way strictly for the lake trout fishing, especially in the beginning of the season when the camp opens.

The larger lakers are usually taken right after ice-out during the first two or three weeks of fishing. Casting and fly fishing opportunities are best then for both trout and silver char. Throughout the season, small lake trout can be taken on ultralight spinning tackle and fly rod in shallow water by sight casting to feeding/cruising pods. This makes for a great afterdinner diversion, and in fact, can be done almost all night long at this time, as it is nearly book-reading light through the late hours.

It is a camp policy to fish with barbless hooks only, prefer-

It's a long way from just about everywhere to the high Arctic region of Victoria Island, where the fishing season lasts just a few weeks and the ground remains permanently frozen up to 6 inches below the surface.

A float plane ferries anglers to good fishing spots on Victoria Island the way a New York City businessperson hops in a taxi to make meetings around town.

ably single hooks on spoons and spinners, and no more than one set of treble hooks on plugs. All but one trophy fish must be released.

Victoria Island has various fishing locales that have not been fished in years, or which have never seen a lure. This is partly due to the fact that some waters here open up only every few years, usually after a mild winter. One such lake apparently yielded an enormous fish a few years ago to a resident angler.

Some of the best arctic char fishing in the world is found on Victoria Island; this large and brightly colored char was caught there in August.

Trophy lake trout, like this 35-pounder, are possible catches in Merkley Lake and some of the other lakes and flowages on Victoria Island.

APPROXIMATELY 600 MILES FROM THE EASTERN UNITED STATES, **BERMUDA** SITS ALONE IN THE WESTERN ATLANTIC OCEAN.

Bermuda beckons many tourists each season, including those who are interested in big-game fishing for tuna and billfish.

BERMUDA

It is variety that makes Bermuda shine as a fishing spot, and this includes the pelagic species as well as the inshore and reef dwellers.

Offshore, the bottom gives way to great depths in between crags, and these features that are plied for such roaming species as marlin, tuna, and wahoo.

The primary fishing is for yellowfin tuna, which are one of the ocean's hardest-fighting sportfish. Bermuda's yellowfin are known as Allison tuna; they don't run large on average, with 25- to 40-pounders the norm. But sometimes there are schools of bigger fish to be had. Most tuna fishing here is done with relatively light tackle. Outfits with 12- to 20-pound line are employed in stand-up fishing, using bait that has been dropped into a chum slick and fighting the tuna from a

stationary boat.

The yellowfin are primarily caught while chumming on the Challenger Bank, which is 15 miles offshore, or the Argus Bank, which is 25 miles offshore. These are pinnacles that are over 150 feet deep. Chum is ladled out and cut or whole bait is fished amidst the chum, which is particularly exciting because fish are hooked close to the boat and are often spotted as they cruise through the chum slick. A wide range of fish are caught by this method, including yellowfin tuna, blackfin tuna, rainbow runner, dolphin, mackerel, and wahoo.

Wahoo are one of Bermuda's foremost fish. Bermuda holds several line-class world records for this species (and also for blackfin tuna), and there is usually an abundance of wahoo on the banks in September and October. Wahoo are usually caught from May on, and many are taken by trolling. Another notable offshore quarry here is amberjack, which have been taken in world-record sizes off Challenger Bank.

Inshore, there are numerous reefs, with opportunity to catch yellowtail snapper, gray snapper, little tunny (bonito), and various jacks by chumming and fishing bait, or by jigging. In the shallows, barracuda and palometa lurk, as do bonefish, although they are difficult for the unguided angler to locate, since there are not many traditional tidal flats areas. The water is deeper than flats anglers are accustomed to, and spotting and stalking tailing bonefish is seldom possible. Nevertheless, these speedsters are caught in Whitney, Long, and Shelly bays, and at Castle Point, with small jigs as the favored offering.

It is worth noting that Bermuda is often a windy locale, with hard-blow days to be experienced at times even during the warmer months.

An angler battles a large Allison, or yellowfin, tuna on the Challenger Banks off Bermuda. These fish are principally caught by anchoring and spreading out a chum slick.

MOST OF **WEST POINT LAKE** LIES IN GEORGIA, BUT IT DOES SPILL OVER INTO ALABAMA. IT IS EASILY REACHED FROM I-85 SOUTH OF ATLANTA AND HAS MANY PUBLIC-ACCESS SPOTS.

Some of the best fishing at West Point, especially in the summer, is had at deep-water humps. This angler was photographed one August day scouring a creek arm for such a locale.

WEST POINT LAKE
Georgia

West Point Lake is not as old as many other southern impoundments, but it is fairly renowned among in-the-know anglers and also noted for having had a series of up-down fisheries since it was created in 1974. Lately it has been on an upswing, and its largemouth bass and hybrid striper fisheries are some of the best in this region.

A 26,000-acre impoundment on the Chattahoochee River, West Point was once loaded with eager bass and in the mid-1980s known for producing giant largemouths, and plenty of them. There is a good population of bass here and still a lot of really big largemouth in this lake, but the trophies do not come to the casual fisherman, nor to the one who probes the banks.

There is not a great deal of cover on those banks, however, there is a lot of submerged timber in deeper water, plus other structure to attract and hold bass. Much timber is along the creek channels, making such locales as Wehadkee, Stroud, Veasey, Whitewater, Yellowjacket, and Maple creeks very popular.

Submerged humps and mounds, roadbeds, and similar hydrographic features are underappreciated places to catch big bass here, and regulars know the location of dozens of such locales, visiting them often, especially in the hot weather of summer, to find if bass have moved in to feed. These locales are primarily fished with deep-diving crankbaits and plastic worms. The worms are dragged ever-so-slowly along the bottom, often using the slow drift of the boat to move them along. A study of contour maps and searching with sonar is necessary to find these locales.

Perhaps the easiest fishing here takes place in the spring, when bass are congregated along points. In the fall they are concentrated and can be caught in bunches on jigging spoons.

West Point has a good population of spotted (Kentucky) bass, which don't grow to the sizes of largemouths, but are aggressive, tenacious fish. It also has the relatively uncommon redeye (or shoal) bass, although not in great numbers. Hybrid stripers provide excitement for anglers who like these stout, hard-pulling creatures.

Largemouth bass have experienced cyclical fluctuations at West Point, but have done well in recent years and are available in sizes larger than this.

PHOTO CREDITS

All photographs by Ken Schultz,
with the following exceptions:
page 74 courtesy Fairfield Bay Marina
page 83 courtesy Mariner Outboards

ACKNOWLEDGMENTS

The author would like to acknowledge the assistance of numerous people, lodge owners, tourism agencies, and others over the years, whose assistance in various ways ultimately lead to the information here and the accompanying photographs.

Special thanks to:

Paul Merzig, President, Paul Merzig's Adventure Safaris, Ltd., Chicago, who represents lodges and outfitters at some of the locales in the book, as well as elsewhere.

Field & Stream, especially Editor Duncan Barnes, for giving me the opportunity to visit various great fishing locales to report on them for the world's number-one sportsman's magazine.

The Canadian Consulate, Tourism Division, in particular Lois Gerber.

The tourism agencies, lodge owners, guides, and other individuals who are listed in the information/contact section of this book.

The anglers who cooperated/assisted in taking the photos used here.

My daughters—Kristen, Alyson, and Megan—who have been patient and understanding while I have been gathering the information needed to do such a project.

CONTACT INFORMATION

Call or write the following places for specific information about destinations (Contact information was correct at time of compilation, the publishers are not responsible for subsequent changes).

1. ALAGNAK RIVER:
Katmai Lodge, 2825 90th S.E., Everett, WA 98204 (206-337-0326).

2. ASHUANIPI RIVER:
Northern Lights Fishing Lodge, P.O. Box 279, Labrador City, Labrador, Canada A2V 2K5 (709-944-5056).

3. ATLIN:
Paul Merzig's Adventure Safaris, Eight S. Michigan Ave., Suite 2012, Chicago, IL 60603 (312-782-4756).

4. ATTAWAPISKAT RIVER:
In Season Adventures, Box 324, Mesick, MI 49668 (616-885-1481).

5. BEAVERKILL RIVER:
Office of Public Information, Sullivan County Government Center, Monticello, NY 12701 (800-343-INFO).

6. BERMUDA:
Bermuda Department of Tourism, Suite 201, 310 Madison Ave., New York, NY 10017. (212-818-9800)

7. BIG SAND LAKE:
Big Sand Lake Lodge, Box 56, Cowan, Manitoba, Canada R0L 0L0 (204-569-4856).

8. BOUNDARY WATERS CANOE AREA:
Minnesota Arrowhead, 734 E. Superior St., Duluth, MN 55802 (218-727-7967).

9. BROADBACK RIVER:
Tourisme Quebec, C.P. 20000, Quebec City, Quebec, Canada G1K 7X2 (800-361-6490).

10. CABO SAN LUCAS:
Mexican Government Tourism Office, 405 Park Ave., Suite 1002, New York, NY 10022 (212-755-7261).

11. CAMPBELL RIVER:
April Point Lodge, P.O. Box 1, Campbell River, BC, Canada V9W 4Z9 (604-285-2222).

12. CHANTREY INLET:
Chantrey Inlet Lodge, P.O. Box 637, Fort France, ON, Canada P9A 1S5 (807-274-3666).

13. COLUMBIA RIVER:
Ed Iman, 525 N.W. 25th, Gresham, OR 97030 (503-667-3945).

14. COZUMEL:
Mexican Government Tourism Office, 405 Park Ave., Suite 1002, New York, NY 10022 (212-755-7261).

15. DELAWARE RIVER:
Brian Wilson, Catskill Angling Adventures, 121 Stockton Ave., Walton, NY 13856 (607-865-7659).

16. ENGLISH RIVER:
Labrador Angling Adventures, Ltd., Awesome Lake Lodge, Box 320, Clarenville, Newfoundland A0E 1J0 (709-466-2413).

17. FLORIDA KEYS:
Chamber of Commerce, Key West, FL 33040. (305-294-2587)

18. FRENCH RIVER:
Art Barefoot, Bear's Den Lodge, Hartley Bay, R.R. 2, Alban, ON, Canada P0M 1A0 (705-857-2757); Peter Schennach, Atwood Island Lodge, 6315 Shawson Dr., Unit 1, Mississauga, ON, Canada L5T 1J2 (416-689-4836).

19. GOUIN RESERVOIR:
Tourisme Quebec, P.O. Box 20000, Quebec City, Quebec, Canada G1K 7X2 (800-443-7000).

20. GREAT BEAR LAKE:
Paul Merzig's Adventure Safaris, Eight S. Michigan Ave., Suite 2012, Chicago, IL 60603 (312-782-4756).

21. GREAT SLAVE LAKE:
Frontier Fishing Lodge, c/o Paul Merzig's Adventure Safaris, Eight S. Michigan Ave., Suite 2012, Chicago, IL 60603 (312-782-4756).

22. GREER'S FERRY LAKE:
Fairfield Bay Resort Center, P.O. Box 3008, Fairfield Bay, AR 72008 (800-643-9790).

23. KAWARTHA LAKES:
Peterborough Kawartha Tourism and Convention Bureau, 135 George St. N., Peterborough, ON, Canada K9H 3R9 (705-742-2201).

24. KENTUCKY AND BARKLEY LAKES:
Land Between the Lakes, Golden Pond, KY 42231 (502-924-5602).

25. KEPIMITS LAKE:
Ashuanipi Fishing and Hunting Camps, P.O. Box 219, Labrador City, Labrador, Canada A2V 2K5 (709-944-5056).

26. LAC BEAUCHENE:
Gary St. George, La Reserve Beauchene, C.P. 910, Temiscamingue, Quebec, Canada J0Z 3R0 (819-627-3865 summer, and 819-627-3308 winter).

27. LAKE ERIE:
Port Clinton Chamber of Commerce, 111 West Perry St., Port Clinton, OH 43452 (419-734-5503).

28. LAKE EUFAULA:
Historic Chattahoochee Commission, P.O. Box 33, Eufaula, AL 36027 (205-687-6664).

29. LAKE GUNTERSVILLE:
Guntersville Chamber of Commerce, P.O. Box 577, Guntersville, AL 35976 (205-582-3612).

30. LAKE KISSIMMEE:
Lake Wales Chamber of Commerce, P.O. Box 191, Lake Wales, FL 33853. (813-676-3445)

31. LAKE MEAD:
Las Vegas News Bureau, Las Vegas Convention Center, Las Vegas, NV 89109 (702-735-3611).

32. LAKE MICHIGAN:
Michigan Travel Bureau, P.O. Box 30226, Lansing, MI 48909. (517-773-0670)

33. LAKE OAHE:
South Dakota Division of Tourism, Box 1000, Pierre, SD 57501 (800-843-1930); Mike McClelland, Fishing Enterprises, P.O. Box 7108, Pierre, SD 57501 (605-224-8599).

34. LAKE OF THE WOODS:
Larry Anderson's Centre Island South, P.O. Box Oak Island, MN 56741; Totem Lodge, P.O. Box 180, Sioux Narrows, ON, Canada P0X 3M9 (807-274-3666).

35. LAKE OKEECHOBEE:
South Florida Water Management District, P.O. Box V, West Palm Beach, FL 33402 (305-686-8800).

36. LAKE ONTARIO:
Gary Edwards, Wild River Inn, P.O. Box 163, Pulaski, NY 13142 (315-298-4459); Bill Kelley, 74 Mayflower St., Rochester, NY 14615 (716-865-0055).

37. LAKE OUACHITA:
Mountain Harbor Resort, Rt. 1, Box 305, Mt. Ida, AR 71957 (501-867-2191).

38. LAKE POWELL:
Del Webb Recreational Properties, P.O. Box 29040, Phoenix, AZ 85038 (602-264-8481).

39. LAKE SAM RAYBURN:
Corps of Engineers, Sam Rayburn Project, Rt. 3, Box 436, Jasper, TX 75951 (409-384-5716).

40. LAKE TEXOMA:
Lake Texoma Association, P.O. Box 610, Kingston, OK 73439 (405-564-2334).

41. MIRAMICHI RIVER:
Old River Lodge, R.R. 2, Doaktown, NB, Canada E0C 1G0 (506-365-2253).

42. MONTAUK:
Montauk Chamber of Commerce, Montauk, NY 11954. (516-668-2428)

43. NIAGARA RIVER:
Bill Hilts, Jr., Niagara County Sportfishing, 59 Park Ave., Lockport, NY 14094. (716-439-6035)

44. NOVA SCOTIA:
Perry Munro, Mountain Maple Lodge, Black River, Kings County, Nova Scotia, Canada B6P 1X6 (902-542-2658); Nova Scotia Department of Tourism, P.O. Box 456, Halifax, NS Canada B3J 2R5 (902-424-5000).

45. NUELTIN LAKE:
Garry Gurke, Nueltin Fly-In Lodges, P.O. Box 1561, Morden, Manitoba, Canada R0G 1J0 (204-822-4143).

46. OTTAWA RIVER:
Lorne Spotswood, Laurentian View Cottages, Westmeath, ON, Canada K0J 2L0 (613-587-4829).

47. RED RIVER:
Bird River Outfitters, 76 Arlington St., Winnipeg, Manitoba, Canada R3G 1Y4 (204-786-7771); Travel Manitoba, 7-155 Carlton St., Winnipeg, Manitoba, Canada R3C 3H8 (800-665-0040).

48. RIVERS INLET:
Rivers Inlet Sportsman Club, c/o Paul Merzig's Adventure Safaris, Eight S. Michigan Ave., Suite 2012, Chicago, IL 60603 (312-782-4756).

49. ST. LAWRENCE RIVER:
Chambers of Commerce, Cape Vincent, NY 13618; Clayton, NY 13624; Alexandria Bay, NY 13607; Jim Brabant, Clayton, NY 13624 (315-686-5118).

50. SAN DIEGO:
Department of Fish and Game, 1416 Ninth St., Sacramento, CA 95814 (916-445-3531).

51. SANTEE-COOPER:
Santee-Cooper Country, Drawer 40, Santee, SC 29142 (800-854-2131).

52. SEA OF CORTEZ:
Mexican Government Tourism Office, 405 Park Ave., Suite 1002, New York, NY 10022 (212-755-7261).

53. SOUTHWESTERN NEW BRUNSWICK:
Bill Ensor, Department of Tourism, C.P. Box 12345, Fredericton, NB, Canada E3B 5C3 (506-453-2444).

54. SQUAM LAKE:
New Hampshire Office of Vacation and Travel, P.O. Box 856, Concord, NH 03301 (603-271-2343).

55. TOLEDO BEND RESERVOIR:
Toledo Bend Tourist Information Center, R.R. 1, Box 781, Many, LA 71449 (318-256-5185).

56. TRUMAN LAKE:
Bucksaw Point Marina, Rt. 3, Box 181, Clinton, MO 64735 (816-477-3313).

57. VICTORIA ISLAND:
High Arctic Lodge, Box 1229, Revelstoke, BC, Canada V0E 2S0 (604-837-2928).

58. WALKER'S CAY:
Walker's Cay Hotel and Marina, 700 S.W. 34th St., Fort Lauderdale, FL 33315 (800-327-3714).

59. WEST POINT LAKE:
Corps of Engineers, P.O. Box 574, West Point, GA 31833 (404-645-2937).

60. WHITE RIVER:
Gaston's White River Resort, One River Rd., Lakeview, AR 72642 (501-431-5202).